Take 10 to Menó

10 Minute Daily Readings thru Colossians

Bill Simpson

The blog of this book can be read online at Take10toMenó.com

Bill also authored *How to Ask God – for What He Wants to Give You*, published 2016, visit HowToAskGod.com

Cover Design: Todd Phelps

DEDICATION

I am honored to dedicate this book to pastors and church leaders all over the world who are striving diligently, by the Lord's wisdom and power, to equip their congregations to do the work of the ministry, to build up the body of Christ, *until we all reach unity in the faith and in the knowledge of God's Son, growing into a mature man with a stature measured by Christ's fullness.* Ephesians 4:13 HCSB

ACKNOWLEDGMENTS

I became a follower of Jesus by God's grace through the ministry of Dr. David Chadwick and the family of Forest Hill Church in Charlotte, NC in 1982. This came after listening to countless seed-sowing sermons from my father-in-law, Rev. C. Paul Jones (while dating his daughter). Dr. Dennis Gill of Community Bible Church was instrumental in guiding us to attend Columbia International University for theological training to prepare for missionary service. My faithful professors at CIU and Reformed Theological Seminary (where I took multiple courses after returning to the states), and our fellow servants at SIM have all been strategic in shaping my understanding of God and how to have a vibrant and authentic relationship with him. I also want to acknowledge the enormous clarity I gained from Dallas Willard's books, especially *The Divine Conspiracy* and *Living in Christ's Presence*.

After returning from our ministry in Senegal, West Africa, I was honored and privileged to pastor two wonderful church families: Community Bible Church in High Point, NC and Manchester Creek Community Church in Rock Hill, SC. I am deeply grateful to both church families for the agape love we received while I served as their Senior Pastor.

CONTENTS

TAKE 10 TO MENÓ

INTRODUCTION

The apostle John, in both his Gospel and his first two letters, repeatedly reminded believers how important it is to remain (abide, continue) in Christ and in his Word. The Greek word is *menó*. Jesus stressed this reality in John 15:1-17, continually stating that his followers must *menó* in him by *menó*-ing in his words and in his love. He made this startling promise: "Those who *menó* in me, and I in them, will produce much fruit. For apart from me you can do nothing."

The purpose of this book is to help the reader remain (*menó*) in Christ by reading a passage of Scripture and then striving to understand how to apply it. Each reading should take at least ten minutes to read. In this book, there are eighteen, ten-minute readings that take the reader through each verse of the apostle Paul's letter to the believers in the church in Colossae.

Thank you for your commitment to *Take 10 to Menó* through this amazingly powerful and practical Epistle. May our Father fill you with the complete knowledge of his will in all wisdom and spiritual understanding so that: the way you live will be worthy of him - fully pleasing him in every way, your life will produce lasting fruit in every good work of faith you pursue, and you will grow more and more in your understanding of God.

TAKE 10 TO MENÓ

READING #1 – FAITH, HOPE & LOVE
COLOSSIANS 1:1-8

[1]Paul, an apostle of Christ Jesus by God's will, and Timothy our brother: [2]To the saints in Christ at Colossae, who are faithful brothers. Grace to you and peace from God our Father. [3]We always thank God, the Father of our Lord Jesus Christ, when we pray for you, [4]for we have heard of your faith in Christ Jesus and of the love you have for all the saints [5]because of the hope reserved for you in heaven. You have already heard about this hope in the message of truth, the gospel [6]that has come to you. It is bearing fruit and growing all over the world, just as it has among you since the day you heard it and recognized God's grace in the truth. [7]You learned this from Epaphras, our dearly loved fellow slave. He is a faithful servant of the Messiah on your behalf, [8]and he has told us about your love in the Spirit. HCSB

1

Read vs4-8 again. Do you see the primary action in this passage? Paul and Timothy *heard* about the faith and love of the Colossians from Epaphras. The Colossians' faith and love came from hearing *about the hope in the message of truth, the gospel* (v5), also from Epaphras. But they didn't just hear what he was teaching, they *recognized God's grace* (v6) in what they heard. They understood God's message of hope in Jesus and learned about his love, and they acted. They believed and received this truth into their lives, entrusting their eternal destiny to this *fantastic news* (this is what the word "gospel" means) and were forever changed.

Think back to how you came to believe. Who was your Epaphras? How many people did God send to help you understand *this hope* (v5), recognize God's grace and accept it? How did God orchestrate the circumstances of your life so that when his *message of truth, the gospel* came to you, you heard and understood it? Take time to thank God for sending that person or those people into your life and for opening the eyes of your heart so that you could understand it and receive it to be *the truth*.

Notice in v4 how Paul heard about their faith and love. I wonder what Epaphras told him? I wonder how they practically expressed their faith and love? Whatever they did, Paul summed it up by writing: *for we have heard of your faith in Christ*

Jesus and of the love you have for all the saints (v4). They weren't missionaries or pastors. They certainly weren't Christian recording artists or authors. The Colossian believers were simple people who experienced the spiritual transformation of coming to believe in Jesus, who is Christ the Messiah ("Christ" is the Greek word, "Messiah" is the Hebrew/Jewish word, both mean "God's Anointed One", "the Savior"). They were ordinary people just like you!

God's desire for you is the same as it was for them. He wants to help you live out your faith in love. According to Jesus, the main characteristic that sets us apart as his followers is that we love *all the saints* (v4). Faith and love are inseparable. They are two sides of the same coin. You will find them paired throughout the Bible because our faith is in the One who *is* love. They are so connected that Paul was led by the Spirit to write this statement: *The only thing that counts is faith expressing itself through love* (Galatians 5:6 NIV). What matters the most in your life is your faith in Christ being lived out through your love for Christ and for his people, *all the saints.*

Nope, "saints" doesn't refer to New Orleans' NFL team. Nor does "saint" refer to great Christians of long ago who now have a statue to honor them or their own cathedral in Europe – although that's how the term is incorrectly used.

"Holy" and "saint" come from the exact same word. You are a saint through your faith in Jesus, because God has set you apart. He calls you a saint because he has made you to be his very son or daughter. He chose you and appointed you to belong to him and he expects you to be faithful to him. Your Father's will for you is to learn how to be fully devoted to him just like Jesus was. This letter to the church in Colossae is all about inspiring you to remain (*menó*) faithful to your Father because of the grace he has shown you and continues to show you. Your faith is best expressed by how you selflessly love other believers, which means you put their wants, needs and interests ahead of your own. This kind of love does not look to be reciprocated and it comes with no strings attached. This kind of love, from the Greek word *agape*, always costs the giver. And agape love is totally impossible to pull off on your own!

Two things will help you in this most difficult undertaking. No, three. Definitely three! First, like the Colossians, focus your heart on *the hope reserved for you in heaven* (v5). "You" is plural. Every follower of Jesus has experienced the same grace from God and we will all live together in a sinless new world, in the visible presence of God, in absolute love and peace. Think about that for a moment. No loneliness or depression, no jealousy or envy, no burdens or sadness, no broken relationships, no cheating, no gossiping... only Jesus' kind of love - agape. That's what is coming for us as his people. Think about the reality of it. Picture it in your mind. Let the most beautiful place you have ever seen or your most cherished relationship remind you of the amazing world that will be your forever home. This world we live in is drenched in sin. Imagine a sinless world!

Secondly, the love you have been given is from God. He is in you through the Holy Spirit. That's why v8 declares: *and he has told us about your love in the Spirit.* You can only love like Jesus loved through the power of his indwelling Spirit within you. Because every believer has the Spirit in them, we also have the same potential to love like he does. Therefore, you never face another believer one on one. That's just not how relationships work in the Kingdom of Jesus. If you and another believer, like your spouse for example, aren't getting along well, realize that the Spirit is in you both. Your arguing means you are not living like the One who lives in both of you. Remember that he loves the other person just as much as he loves you. So stop taking yourself so seriously. Agape love by learning to listen so that you truly hear the other person's heart.

Third, because you are in the Spirit and the Spirit is in you, rely on him when your emotions get the best of you. When you feel jealousy, rejection or anger towards another follower of Jesus, and it happens all the time, acknowledge your sin and ask the Father to strengthen you. His power can prevent you from saying something that you'll later regret. By his strength, you can reject focusing on what is wrong with the other person. Stop replaying the DVD and definitely don't tweet or post about how you feel! Instead, ask God to help you focus on what is lacking *in you*. Ask him to strengthen your faith to work itself out in Christ's agape love. The Spirit of Jesus is your helper who is in you, 24/7. Rely upon him!

Take Action:

- Keep reminding yourself that the Father made you able to see and believe what you never deserved to know.

- Thank God throughout the day for making you one of his saints. Every time you encounter a non-believer, thank God that he has given you faith to believe.

- Look for how God's grace is working through you to love others during the course of each day. Ask your Father to increase your *love in the Spirit* (v8) in everything you do.

READING #2 – KINGDOM COME PRAYING
COLOSSIANS 1:9-14

9For this reason also, since the day we heard this, we haven't stopped praying for you. We are asking that you may be filled with the knowledge of His will in all wisdom and spiritual understanding, 10so that you may walk worthy of the Lord, fully pleasing to Him, bearing fruit in every good work and growing in the knowledge of God. 11May you be strengthened with all power, according to His glorious might, for all endurance and patience, with joy 12giving thanks to the Father, who has enabled you to share in the saints' inheritance in the light. 13He has rescued us from the domain of darkness and transferred us into the kingdom of the Son He loves. 14We have redemption, the forgiveness of sins, in Him. HCSB

Read vs13-14 one more time. Let the power and the profundity of these truths soak over you. The Father of your Lord Jesus Christ has personally rescued you from the rule and reign of the dark world in this life and in the life to come. There are only two worlds – two kingdoms. Every person on the planet is either in one or the other. You *were* in the other. But by God's amazing grace and through your faith in Jesus, you are a permanent member of the Son's kingdom, fully forgiven of every sin, past, present and future. "Redemption" is a Greek word from the first century that was a legal term describing a slave who had been freed by a ransom payment. Was your ransom paid for by your acts of kindness or good looks? Of course not. You have redemption *in Him*.

The Kingdom has come to you. It is in you. You bring the Kingdom wherever you go. And you have been instructed by Jesus to ask the Father to make his kingdom come more and more *in* you and *through* you. That is the first request in Jesus' prayer outline he gave to his followers in Luke 11. Jesus' prayer outline has five points: 1st - Praise and thank the Father, 2nd - Ask for his kingdom to come, 3rd - Ask for the tangible things you need, 4th - Confess your sins and forgive everyone who owes you anything, and 5th - Acknowledge his presence and power to protect you. Notice that the very first request Jesus instructed his followers to ask his Father was to make the Kingdom come. That's why God gave us prayers like Colossians 1:9-12. It is a "Kingdom Come Prayer".

There are two things we are to ask the Father to do from this prayer. The first one is in v9: *that you may be filled with the knowledge of his will in all wisdom and spiritual understanding.* God wants you to continually ask him to fill your mind and heart so that you will know what he wants you to say and do — *the knowledge of his will.* Understanding God's will means you have been given wisdom and insights by his Spirit into your spirit. The Spirit takes God's truths, that come to you in reading the Bible, from sermons, songs, books, poems, experiences, etc. and he opens the eyes of your heart to be able to comprehend and apply those truths. Being filled with the full knowledge of God's will is an on-going need because he has created all kinds of wonderful things for you to do that will produce lasting fruit (Ephesians 2:10).

The Spirit knows everything you will need to know today. He knows all of God's truths, which include quantum physics, nuclear fission, the weather and every intention of each person you will interact with today and tonight. Because he knows everything about everything, what you need more than anything is the Spirit's help. With his wisdom and insights, you will know how to navigate through your day so that what you think, say and do will please your Father in the heavens.

The three results of asking him to fill you with deeper understanding of his will are found in v10: 1st *so that you may walk worthy of the Lord, fully pleasing to Him*, 2nd so that you will bear *fruit in every good work*, and 3rd so that you will grow in your *knowledge of God*. Read those three results again! Isn't that the life you really want? Don't you want to live so that your choices please God? Don't you want to do things that will make a lasting impact for the Kingdom? Don't you want to understand God better? Then ask, and keep on asking for him to fill you up to the brim with the full knowledge of his will in every situation and circumstance. This is exactly how I began writing this devotional, asking the Father to fill my mind with understanding of how I can explain this passage so that it honors him and inspires you.

When you aren't sure what to say or how to react, pause and fire up this flare prayer. Ask your glorious and loving, heavenly Father to give you all the wisdom and spiritual insights you need to respond so that he is pleased and so that fruit abounds. As you keep asking and experiencing his help, you will grow closer to him, understanding him more completely as you grow in your knowledge of God.

The second request in this prayer is equally as practical to your daily schedule: *11May you be strengthened with all power, according to His glorious might.* Whoa! How much power does he have available for you? How much strength do you need each day? If you are not in the habit of asking God to give you his power throughout your day, you are about to experience an entirely new life-dynamic. Once you begin regularly asking him to empower you with his strength, you will never stop. And you will learn how desperately dependent on him you actually are. And that, my friend, is the most important reality for you to grasp today. You need his power in you more than you will ever realize. Once you begin to experience the Father strengthening you, you will grow closer to him and your life will have more purpose, joy and meaning.

Look what's going to happen as you ask and keep on asking the Father to empower you with his unlimited strength: you will be given *all endurance and patience, with joy 12giving thanks to the Father, who has enabled you to share in the saints' inheritance in the light.* His power in you will make you able to endure every difficult situation that the world can throw at you. His strength working in you will give you the patience you need for the most challenging person in your network of influence, even those terrible drivers you face each day. In the midst of tough times, his power can keep your joy secure because it will be based on the fact that you belong in his kingdom since he took the initiative. These results can be yours, each and every day, as you continue (*menó*) asking your Father to strengthen you with all power according to his glorious might.

Take Action:

- Begin using this prayer after each daily reading, taking time to talk to your Father about the ways you need his knowledge and power.

- Develop the habit of using "flare prayers" to ask God to give you understanding or strength in the heat of the battle.

- As you interact with non-believers, remind yourself that they are still captive to the dark world. Ask the Father to rescue them like he rescued you. Be available to tell them about the hope you have in Jesus.

For further reading about this prayer and the other Kingdom Come Prayers, pick up a copy of my book, *How to Ask God - for What He Wants to Give You* at www.HowToAskGod.com

READING #3 – JESUS IS...
COLOSSIANS 1:15-20

15*He is the image of the invisible God,*

the firstborn over all creation.

16*For everything was created by Him,*

in heaven and on earth,

the visible and the invisible,

whether thrones or dominions

or rulers or authorities —

all things have been created through Him and for Him.

[17]*He is before all things,*

and by Him all things hold together.

[18]*He is also the head of the body, the church;*

He is the beginning,

the firstborn from the dead,

so that He might come to have

first place in everything.

[19]*For God was pleased to have*

all His fullness dwell in Him,

[20]*and through Him to reconcile*

everything to Himself

by making peace

through the blood of His cross —

whether things on earth or things in heaven. HCSB

Did your mind just drift as you read? If so, try reading the passage one more time and focus on each phrase of this majestic description of Jesus. The passage is written in poetic form because it is believed to have been used as a song of praise. Notice how the passage describes who Jesus is rather than what he did. Remember, your faith is in *who* Jesus is, the Lord, the Son of God. Your salvation, that you belong to his kingdom, was made possible by what he did.

Spend these next few minutes thinking about the One in whom you have placed your faith and entrusted your life and eternity. He is the invisible God made visible. God revealed a lot about himself in the Old Testament. But he is seen in Ultra vivid HD clarity in Jesus Christ in the New Testament. Everything we couldn't comprehend about God is made clear to us in the man, Jesus Christ. That's why Hebrews 1:3 declares: *The Son is the radiance of God's glory and the exact expression of His nature…*

The word "firstborn" (v15) means that Jesus holds the place of highest honor and dignity, not that he was the first person created. Jesus has always existed and because he created all things, he is to *have first place in everything* (v18). Your objective today is to live like Jesus is first in everything you do. Remind yourself of that truth throughout your waking hours.

In v16, the word "For" that begins the verse, carries the idea "because". Jesus is head over all of creation because he is the Creator of all things, seen and unseen. Everything that exists was created - check out these next words - *through* Jesus and *for* Jesus. The visible and invisible worlds weren't only created *by* him, they were created *for* him. That is why he loves you so much. You were created *by* him and you were created *for* him. The God of the cosmos treasures his relationship with you. His desire is that you live your life through him and for him. Living your life *for* God will bring you the greatest fulfillment and pleasure possible. This is what Jesus meant when he said that he came to give you an abundant life (John 10:10).

After creating the cosmos, Jesus didn't kick back to watch the show. He is constantly sustaining his creation. In v17 we learn that he holds it all together. That's why nations haven't nuked each other out of existence. A giant meteor hasn't crashed into planet earth because Jesus is keeping all of the galaxies in order, controlling every planet's orbit and rotation. He orders the orbit of planets and protons! He is in absolute control even though evil seems to run rampant throughout our world. But evil's influence is only to the degree that Jesus allows.

The domain of darkness (v13) is on a leash that is firmly held by Christ so you don't have to be afraid of Satan and his demonic forces. They are very real but they are under Jesus' absolute authority. You don't have to worry if some rogue nation is going to launch a nuclear missile, if there will be another school shooting today or a terrorist attack tomorrow. Do not be afraid! Jesus is in firm control of both worlds. When news stories make you fearful or anxious, remind yourself of this passage. Yes, terrible things happen every day. But the Lord Jesus Christ is in absolute control. Our world is broken beyond repair, but he reigns over it for his purposes and he will right every wrong when he returns. When you can't understand why he would allow such awful things to happen, remember that his ways are infinitely higher than your ways. You are incapable of understanding all that Jesus is doing.

But what about your life? Is Jesus really in full control of your world too? Yes, yes, yes! It doesn't feel like it at times, we all experience that. But you must believe that Jesus is exactly who this passage says he is, the head of his Church, which means he is the head of every person who belongs to him. Jesus' resurrection began an entirely new age that was foretold in the Old Testament and will come to complete fruition when he returns. Until that day, Jesus is holding together the lives of every one of his followers. Even though it may feel like things are falling apart, they are not. He holds it all together for his purposes.

The fullness of God dwells in Jesus. Through the blood of his cross, he reconciled you to his Father. You now have peace with God through your faith in his Son. He is preeminent in everything. You are a new creation in Christ because he has made you to be his very own and he is holding your life together by his limitless power. As you think more and more about who Jesus is, it will become easier for you to give him first place in every area of your life.

Your rebellious choices that were opposed to God were reconciled by God himself. Since you chose to sin against him, he was the only one who could secure your forgiveness. Think about that today and tonight, each time you have a jealous urge, an angry thought, whenever you struggle forgiving someone and when your Me Monster shows up. Confess those self-centered acts and rest in the fact of who Jesus is, God the Son, your Savior and your Lord.

Take Action:

- Continue using the prayer in vs9-12 (pg.7), during your devotion times and as flare prayers.

- Look for ways that you can recognize Jesus' control over your life's circumstances, in the news locally and globally, and in nature.

READING #4 – A GIANT BUT
COLOSSIANS 1:21-23

21*Once you were alienated and hostile in your minds because of your evil actions.* 22*But now He has reconciled you by His physical body through His death, to present you holy, faultless, and blameless before Him -* 23*if indeed you remain grounded and steadfast in the faith and are not shifted away from the hope of the gospel that you heard. This gospel has been proclaimed in all creation under heaven, and I, Paul, have become a servant of it.* HCSB

In Reading #3 from 1:15-20, the passage declared who Jesus is. In these verses, Paul wrote about who humans are and what Jesus did about it. His description of people as being *alienated and hostile* includes every person who has ever lived, except of course for Jesus. It's helpful to think about passages like this one in the first person. Read these three verses again in first person by replacing "you" and "your" with "I", "me" and "my". If it helps, use your name instead of the pronouns. Did that help you to better grasp your former and current relationship with the Lord?

Without Christ, you were separated from God because your thinking was completely contrary to his, which made your actions evil. You probably never consider yourself to be alienated from God nor did you think you were his enemy. Regardless of how you felt, you were most definitely estranged from him because your mind and your will were in full agreement to pursue a life that centered itself on you, rather than on him. That is the basis of alienation with God.

Do people you know consider themselves to be separated and estranged from God or hostile towards him in their thoughts and actions? Probably not. God said that the Evil One has blinded their eyes so that they can't understand their true condition (2 Cor 4:4). Most people think they are good to go with the Man upstairs. Didn't you? What they need is to have the eyes of their hearts opened so that they can understand who Jesus is, who they are without him and place their trust in him, just like you did. As you interact with people who don't yet believe Jesus is

Lord and King, pray for God to open their hearts and minds and be ready to tell them about the hope you have in Christ. So tell your story.

The giant "But" in v22 makes all the difference. *But now He has reconciled you...* is the most important truth you will ever embrace. Because you were separated from God and evil in your thinking and doing, the only way things could be made right between you and God was if God did it himself. He alone could heal your relationship because you didn't have the ability to do it on your own. However, he couldn't just forget about your rebellion or forgive all your sins like nothing ever happened. Because God is completely just and holy, your evil had to be punished. Just like a judge can't bang the gavel and declare a convicted felon to be forgiven of his crimes, God could not simply wave his hand and forgive you either. God's very character demands absolute justice. *He has reconciled you by His physical body through His death...* (v22).

Spend time thinking about the fact that God initiated your reconciliation. He not only sent his Son to suffer for you, he opened your heart to receive this truth and gave you faith so that you would believe him. Isn't that amazing? Did you deserve this kind of grace from God? Of course not. But he was thrilled to give you faith so that you would respond by believing and be re-united with him forever.

And there is more to your reconciliation. When your time comes to go home, or if Jesus returns while you're still living on earth, he will present you to his Father *holy, faultless, and blameless* (v22). Notice who is doing the presenting. Who is making whom holy, blameless and without a single flaw? Jesus will present *you* to his Father! Maybe he'll say something like, "Abba, here is my brother/sister who is completely holy, with no faults or sins and who cannot be blamed for anything, because he/she belongs to me." That is the unwavering security of your position with God in Christ. You are holy like Jesus because his holiness covers all of your un-holiness. Every single debit on your spiritual balance statement has been wiped away. Not only that, your account has been credited with the same riches that Jesus possesses.

It's been said that every follower of Jesus needs to preach the gospel to themselves every day. How can you keep the reality of your reconciliation in the forefront of your thinking? The reason it is so important to constantly remind yourself of who you are in Christ is because that is the source of your true joy. Knowing you have been given peace with God and that no one can take it away defines who you are. Unless…

This passage comes with a strong warning (v23). You are secure in Christ if you continue (*menó*) trusting in him and in him alone for peace with God. You must stand firm on the fantastic news (*the gospel*) and not waver. Does this mean that you are earning God's grace by being faithful? Nope. Standing firm means that you are proving that you really do belong to him. You've probably wondered about people who have left the faith. They did not continue (*menó*) with Jesus. By abandoning their faith in Christ, they proved that they never really belonged to him. True faith is always persevering faith. You may stumble, even stumble hard, but you will not fall flat on your face. You will remain (*menó*) with Jesus.

You have had times of unbelief. We all have them. Sometimes our faith shrinks. You've probably had moments when you questioned if all this stuff about Jesus is true. When others have challenged your beliefs, you've likely struggled with your own convictions. In those times, faith has to overcome feelings. Belief is strengthened by the Author of your faith. So cry out to the Lord like the doubting dad did in Mark 9:24: "*Help my unbelief!*".

Perseverance is the reason the prayer requests in v9 and v11 are so critical to *menó*-ing with Jesus.

You need to be filled with the understanding of God's will and you need to be strengthened by his power every day and night if you are going to remain grounded, like the deep roots of a tall tree. The famous line from that classic hymn is so true: "Prone to wander Lord I feel it, prone to leave the God I love. Here's my heart Lord, take and seal it, seal it for thy courts above."

You know what weakness feels like. You know what it does to you when you doubt God. You also know what or who causes you to drift. Identify the people, habits, activities or lack of activities (like prayer, fellowship, worship, giving and serving) that cause you to veer. Identify those things and jettison them. Don't ever stop asking for your Father's help. You will grow stronger and stronger in your faith as you continually remember your desperate dependence on God – the Father, the Son and the Spirit.

Take Action:

- Use the prayer in 1:9-12 (pg.7) as you think about staying true to your faith in Jesus.

- Look for new ways to thank God for reconciling you to himself. Remember, obedience is the proof of your love and devotion to God.

- Strive to be reconciled to everyone, especially those who don't deserve it.

READING #5 – YOU KNOW HIS SECRET
COLOSSIANS 1:24-29

24Now I rejoice in my sufferings for you, and I am completing in my flesh what is lacking in Christ's afflictions for His body, that is, the church. 25I have become its servant, according to God's administration that was given to me for you, to make God's message fully known, 26the mystery hidden for ages and generations but now revealed to His saints. 27God wanted to make known among the Gentiles the glorious wealth of this mystery, which is Christ in you, the hope of glory. 28We proclaim Him, warning and teaching everyone with all wisdom, so that we may present everyone mature in Christ. 29I labor for this, striving with His strength that works powerfully in me. HCSB

Does it strike you as being a little strange how the Spirit inspired Paul to refer to Jesus as God's *mystery*? He used this word to describe Jesus and the gospel (the fantastic news) twenty times in his various letters. Paul used this word because Jesus used the same word. When the twelve disciples asked why he spoke in so many parables, Jesus replied: *"The secret of the kingdom of God has been given to you, but to those outside, everything comes in parables..."* (Mark 4:11). "Mystery" and "secret" are the same Greek word. This mystery that had been kept secret for thousands of years was revealed to the world in the life, crucifixion and resurrection of Jesus Christ. Let this reality soak into your brain: you have been shown the secret of who Jesus is by the grace of God through the work of the Spirit opening the eyes of your heart. This is truly amazing grace!

Instead of trying to earn more of God's favor and grace once we have been shown the mystery, our lives must be about thanking him for letting us in on the secret. You can never earn more of his love through your attempts to be a good follower of Jesus. Obeying his commands is how you demonstrate your love for Jesus. That's how love for God is expressed; through your obedience to his words. Jesus said; "If you love Me, keep my commands (John 14:15, HCSB). Let gratitude, not entitlement, be your on-going response to his amazing grace.

The mystery goes even further because it encompasses everything about faith in Jesus. Look at v27 again. Part of the mystery of the gospel is that Jesus reconciles sinners to God *and* to one another. We can't even imagine how wide the chasm was between the Jews and every other race (*Gentile* meant any non-Jew). As you read previously in v20 (pg.14), Jesus' blood sacrifice on the cross created peace between you and God, and between you and every other believer. All followers of Jesus are now one in him. This is a sweeping doctrine of God that must be embraced so that in the Church (the saints worldwide) and in every local church, we can end partiality, biases and prejudices. We are all *saints* first and foremost. Your nationality, heritage, ethnicity, education, employment, etc. no longer identify who you are, at least it shouldn't. First and foremost, you are a new creation in Christ with a new identity and so is every other follower of Jesus. Therefore, every time you feel partiality of any kind towards another believer - either superiority or inferiority - confess your wrong thinking and ask your Father to fill you with the full knowledge of his will so that you can see yourself, and everyone else, from his perspective.

Another compelling part of the mystery is that the Lord Jesus Christ is *in* you (v27). "Wait! Isn't it the Spirit who is in me?" Glad you asked. He is. But because he and the Father and Jesus exist in such unity, the Bible unequivocally states that Christ is in you when in fact it is actually the Spirit of Christ who is in you. Instead of getting a migraine trying to figure that out, simply rest in the reality of it. But wait, there's more!

Not only is Christ in you, you have the *hope of glory*. That means you have the absolute certainty that when this life is over, you will join Jesus in your real life, a life in paradise in the stunning glory of his visible presence. The Bible tells us that the Spirit is our guarantee of this sure hope (Ephesians 1:13-14). He's your ticket in and you can't lose that ticket! Every time you face your own mortality, remind yourself of this absolute reality and let the hope of your coming glory replace your fear of death and dying.

Thinking about Paul's ministry in this passage will help you better understand God's plans for your role in the Kingdom. God chose Paul to be a very special ambassador for the Kingdom and part of his ministry meant that he would suffer greatly. Paul was often beaten and imprisoned. That was part of God's plan for Paul. Life in Christ by no means guarantees health, wealth and comfort. Don't be confused when you face hard times and people make fun of you because of your allegiance to Jesus. It's part of life in the Kingdom. You will have plenty of difficulties (John 16:33) but you will never face one hardship alone. He is with you and he is in you. And God has a unique plan for every one of his children. Some suffer more than others. Some followers have it easier than others. Don't waste your time and energy comparing.

Paul wrote that God gave him the ministry to teach and preach so that the message of Jesus would be *fully known* (v25). Paul was so passionate and driven that he lived as if Jesus was going to return at any moment. And he never ministered in his own strength. As he wrote in v29, his insatiable drive to help believers become mature in Christ was fueled by the powerful strength of God working in and through him.

You were not chosen by God to be an apostle like Paul. But you were just as "chosen" as Paul was, and you were created to do the work of ministry that God has appointed for *you*. Through your vocation, in your family, among your network of contacts, with your abilities and Spiritual giftedness, you need to be continually strengthened by the Spirit to do your God-given work of ministry. This is why it is so important for you to own the two prayer requests in 1:9-12 (pg.7).

To become mature and live each day in devotion to the Lord, you must be continually infused with his understanding and empowered by his strength. So ask him for both and keep on asking throughout each day. Do the things that God has uniquely gifted and enabled you to do in his power and with the wisdom and insights he gives you through his Spirit. If you need help understanding what your ministry should be, schedule a time to visit with your pastor or one of the other staff members or church leaders. Part of becoming mature in Christ is serving in the Kingdom according to how God has wired you. Never compare how you serve in the Kingdom with how others serve. You are unique to God and so are your kingdom responsibilities.

Do you want to know God's will for your life? Here it is: grow to be mature in Christ! Look at v28 again. Paul's goal through his teaching was to help every believer become mature in Christ. Like those first believers, you are meant for the same purpose. Therefore, it is essential to understand the basics of maturity in Christ. Your spiritual maturity is diametrically opposed to your emotional and physical maturity.

In this life, growing up to be mature is all about becoming independent and self-sufficient. A mature adult no longer relies on their parents. But in Christ, it's just the opposite because the more spiritually mature you become, the more *dependent* you learn to be on your Father. That's why many believers struggle with becoming *mature in Christ*. The more you understand and accept your weaknesses, the more you will depend on the power of God. The more you accept that you don't know it all, the more you'll realize your need for God to give you his wisdom and understanding. Celebrate and rest in your desperate dependence on God because that's how you become mature in Christ. After all, he let you in on his secret!

Take Action:

- Use the prayer in 1:9-12 (pg.7) as you practice becoming more mature in Christ.

- Think about ministry as your regular interactions with people. How are you bringing the Kingdom into those relationships. Also, how do you most enjoy serving in your church?

- Identify and jettison anything that prevents you from growing in your maturity in Christ. What do you need to add to your routine in order to grow in maturity. How are you practicing daily dependence on God?

READING #6 – HE KNOWS EVERYTHING
COLOSSIANS 2:1-5

[1]For I want you to know how great a struggle I have for you, for those in Laodicea, and for all who have not seen me in person. [2]I want their hearts to be encouraged and joined together in love, so that they may have all the riches of assured understanding and have the knowledge of God's mystery - Christ. [3]All the treasures of wisdom and knowledge are hidden in Him. [4]I am saying this so that no one will deceive you with persuasive arguments. [5] For I may be absent in body, but I am with you in spirit, rejoicing to see how well ordered you are and the strength of your faith in Christ. HCSB

Read v3 again. Read it one more time. God has revealed to you his secret, who is the Lord Jesus, and in him are the richest treasures of wisdom and understanding. Try not to have an aneurism over this reality. Jesus knows everything about everything and everyone. He knows all the details of your life and everything that *has* happened, *is* happening and – get this – *is going* to happen to you. Multiply that by the billions of people that are alive today! Jesus owns all the storehouses of wisdom and insights in our world and in the spirit world. That's a lot of data! And he knows all that we don't yet know. Therefore, everything you need to know to live a full and fulfilled life is known by Christ. So tap into that vast treasury of rich knowledge and wisdom.

The radical mind renewal that you need is to realize how Jesus knows more about life than the world does. Think about this example. Do you try to eat healthy? It's a big deal now. The food industry has created all kinds of new revenue opportunities through our desire to eat healthy: organic, all natural, gluten free, grass fed, free range, whole grain, and the categories go on and on. Why do you want to eat healthy? What is healthy for you? How can you know the labels are accurate? More importantly, do you worry about eating healthy because you are afraid of getting cancer or some other disease?

You can drive yourself crazy trying to figure out the best foods to eat. You can easily get off-balance by focusing too much on healthy eating. Who really knows how you should eat and exercise? Jesus does. He is the only one who knows everything about your past, present and future. Your health food store clerk has no idea of your metabolic make-up. The internet certainly doesn't. Your trainer is clueless about your specific muscle, tendon and cartilage condition. But Jesus knows it all.

Imagine if you begin to rely on Jesus' vast treasure of wisdom and knowledge to guide your every decision. That's right, *every* decision. Jesus can give you all the wisdom you need to do your job well, raise your children, to make the best investments, to know who to date, who not to date, where to go to school and what to study. How do you tap into this treasury of wisdom and knowledge? Ask! Then ask again. Don't ever stop asking. Build into your daily routine the habit of relying on the Spirit of Jesus to guide your spirit with his wisdom so that you can make the wisest decisions in every area of your life.

Ask according to God's Word in 1:9 (pg.7). "Father in the heavens, I ask you to fill me with the full knowledge of your will in all wisdom and spiritual understanding about how I should respond to this email." Flare prayers like this one are the key to you learning the wisdom of Christ. The results of this kind of praying to the Father are spelled out in 1:10. You will live your life each day in such a way that it will be worthy of a

35

person who has been shown the mystery of Jesus. You will fully please your Father, who cares about every detail of your day. You will make wise choices and do the kinds of good deeds that will produce lasting results, delicious fruit. And most importantly, you will increase in your full knowledge and understanding of God.

Paul reminded the believers in the church in Colossae that he was struggling for their faith and suffering in countless ways. But for him, it was all worth it because he was convinced that his teaching and writing would bind them all together in love, deepen their understanding of God's glorious grace (v2) and strengthen their faith (v5). God's purpose for you reading this same, 2,000 year-old letter is no different. He preserved it so that you, and all of his adopted children, could read it and understand his truth. He longs for you and your church family, your small group and all of your believing friends to *have all the riches of assured understanding and have the knowledge of God's mystery – Christ.*

You are doing the very thing that will make all of this happen in you. You are feeding your soul on God's Word. Since Jesus is the treasure chest of all wisdom and knowledge, every word he spoke and every word he inspired others to write are the primary outlet for you to grow in the assurance of your understanding of how to apply God's truths to your circumstances. You will not gain this assurance by osmosis. He gave you his Word for you to read it and think about it and strive to understand it so that you can live it out each day. You are doing his very will by taking time to read his Word so that you can better understand it and more faithfully apply it. Congratulations!

This is what is going to happen as you continue (*menó*) in Jesus' teaching. Your understanding about God will be enriched, which will make your love for his people deepen, which will strengthen your faith in Christ. You will *not* be persuaded to believe things that are not true about God, even though they sound compelling. You will be able to discern what is true as you continue to feed your mind and soul and as you commit to living in desperate dependence on the Father, the Son and the Spirit. You will be able to recognize God's values and ethics that are counter to the world's. You will live a life that is pleasing to the Father and inspiring to everyone you know.

Everyone in your network of influence will *see how well ordered you are and the strength of your faith in Christ* (v5). Make that one of your life's goals, to live a strong and orderly life in Christ, by his grace and strength. Not so you can beat your chest and declare, "Look at me! I'm holy!" Your motivation comes from your gratefulness to God. He revealed his mystery to you! Cultivate within your inner most being an attitude of gratitude and you will leave a legacy that will produce eternal results that will make you and your Father smile.

Now may the God of hope fill you with all joy and peace as you believe in Him so that you may overflow with hope by the power of the Holy Spirit. (Romans 15:13, HCSB)

Take Action:

- Before you ask God to fill you according to 1:9 (pg.7), think about the results of this request in 1:10 and how you will apply those today.

- How might you encourage other believers to take at least 10 minutes each day to feed their soul and renew their mind? Consider asking God, at the beginning of each day, to direct you to one person that you can encourage by sharing what you are learning.

- As you face decisions about your work, finances, relationships, school and life in general, ask the Father to fill your mind with his wisdom. Build this practice into your normal routine and keep a record of how he answers those requests.

READING #7 – LIVING IN CHRIST TODAY
COLOSSIANS 2:6-7

⁶Therefore, as you have received Christ Jesus the Lord, walk in Him, ⁷rooted and built up in Him and established in the faith, just as you were taught, overflowing with gratitude. HCSB

The Bible talks a lot about our "walk". It was a common figure of speech used to describe how people lived and conducted their lives. Since the primary form of transportation in those days was walking, it was a perfect metaphor to describe how a person lived. In v6, you are instructed to "walk the talk". If you say you are a follower of Jesus, then live the kind of life that demonstrates your allegiance to him.

When you come across the word "therefore" in the Scriptures, you'll want to understand what it's there for. Paul meant that the reason we're to live the way he described in vs6-7 is because of what he wrote in the preceding verses. You'll recall that he wrote about how every follower of Jesus had been shown God's mystery and given faith to believe it. The "therefore" points back to why you are to live in full devotion to Jesus. Your desire to obey his commands is grounded in the amazing grace that the God of the galaxies has lavished (and continues to lavish) on you.

That is made even more clear in the phrase that follows the "Therefore": *as you have received Christ Jesus the Lord.* How did you receive him? Was it because of your keen sense of humor and magnetic charm? Not quite, huh? The only reason you could understand who Jesus is and put your faith in him is because God chose to reveal that truth to you. You received the knowledge of the mystery of God by his grace, undeserved and unearned. Think about this statement: You received Jesus by grace so live in him every day by that same grace. The definition of "grace" is: you get to think, say and do things that you would never think, say or do without God's direct help.

Think back to yesterday. What did you think, say or do that was directly influenced by the Spirit of Jesus living in you? Or what did another believer think, say or do to you or for you? The way to grow in your gratitude of his constant grace is to develop a sharper sense of recognizing when you are in the flow of that grace. When you recognize it, take the time to thank God for what he just did in, through or for you.

Did you speak a kind word to the cashier? Thank him that you just lived the same way that you received Christ – by his grace. Did you feel compassion or mercy for someone? Thank your heavenly Father for his grace that moved you to exercise *your love in the Spirit* (1:8). Did another follower encourage you? Thank him for loving you through the other saint. As you see God working in and through you in little ways during your day, you will grow in your understanding of him.

Let's jump back into the passage for today. The kind of life you are to live in Christ is vividly described in v7 with several picture words:

· *rooted* – having been firmly rooted or to cause to take root. Jesus is the life-giving soil, watered and full of nutrients, that causes your roots to grow deep. Picture the tallest tree you know of and imagine its strong root system.

· *built up* – being built up, like a house or building. Christ is the foundation of your life on which you build all of your decisions, choices and on which God builds you up. Picture a strong foundation that is the base of a building that can withstand tornadoes and hurricanes.

· *established* – to make firm, confirm or make sure. God is making your faith more and more certain, sure and steadfast, as you feed your mind. Picture your faith in Christ like the rising sun. It rises with absolute certainty every day, whether, or weather, you can see it or not.

· *overflowing* – to abound, to have more than enough with leftovers. This word describes your gratitude. Remember back to when you had a delicious meal with so much fantastic food you couldn't begin to eat it all, even though you tried.

Your Father wants you to live each day by being firmly rooted and grounded in Christ: in your knowledge *about* him and in your faith *in* him. His will is for you to be firm and certain about all of your beliefs in Jesus, which means you are understanding his Word and regularly applying it correctly to your life's circumstances. From the grace God is lavishing on you, your gratitude should overflow in abundance, splashing out on those around you.

What a really cool picture of spiritual growth! But is that how your life is actually going? Maybe not. It's not like every day is so euphoric that others have to slap the smile off of your face. Life, as you well know, is hard. This verse describes how you are to face the good days and the difficult days, the fun times and the heart-breaking losses. Jesus never promised you an easy, care-free life. He did promise that you would never go through the tough times alone. He promised to strengthen you and to embolden your faith, as you remain (*menō*) in him.

So what do you need to do to become more rooted and built up in Jesus? Ask your Father that very question. Ask and keep asking. Seek the council of more mature believers who are living orderly and faithful lives. Learn to pray for yourself and for others using the requests like Paul used in 1:9-12 (pg.7) and in Ephesians 1:17-19; 3:16-19 and Philippians 1:9-11.

"But seek first the kingdom of God and His righteousness, and all these things (everything you need in life) *will be provided to you."* (Matthew 6:33)

Take Action:

- Take time to think about what you are truly putting first in your life. What or who is an idol?

- Use Jesus' outline for praying (Luke 11:1-5) by first asking for Kingdom come requests (1:9-12) then for your physical needs. Confess your sins and forgive everyone who owes you anything.

READING #8 – YOU'VE GOT CREDENTIALS
COLOSSIANS 2:8-15

8See to it that no one takes you captive by philosophy and empty deceit, according to human tradition, according to the elemental spirits of the world, and not according to Christ. 9For in him the whole fullness of deity dwells bodily, 10and you have been filled in him, who is the head of all rule and authority. 11In him also you were circumcised with a circumcision made without hands, by putting off the body of the flesh, by the circumcision of Christ, 12having been buried with him in baptism, in which you were also raised with him through faith in the powerful working of God, who raised him from the dead. 13And you, who were dead in your trespasses and the uncircumcision of your flesh, God made alive together with him, having forgiven us all our trespasses, 14by canceling the record of debt that stood against us with its legal demands. This he set aside, nailing it to the cross. ¹⁵*He disarmed the rulers and authorities and put them to open shame, by triumphing over them in him.* ESV

Picture in your mind what your email signature would look like if your name was followed by all the initials you ever imagined. What new opportunities might those qualifications create for you. Don't just picture the initials from degrees and certifications, include vocational initials like VP or CFO. If you had every credential you ever wanted, how much better would life be? How would it feel to have all of those initials attached to *your* name? How might those letters change your financial status?

Now wake-up and return to reality! You read in 1:13 (pg.7) that your Father, because you believe his Son, has rescued you from the kingdom of darkness and planted you into the kingdom of his beloved Son. Remember that one? There are only two kingdoms in the universe, and that includes both the visible and the spiritual worlds. There are only two! Because those initials you just considered do not belong to the kingdom of Jesus, they are part of the kingdom of darkness. They aren't necessarily bad and if you have them, you most likely worked and studied very hard to earn those initials. But you must realize that those initials determine who is important and who isn't. Those initials are the primary way that our society determines a person's value and that kind of thinking is most definitely from the dark domain.

The amazing reality of God's kingdom is this: These verses affirm that you have been fully credentialed with the highest qualifications that exist in both worlds. Your credentialing is confirmed by three little prepositions: *by*, *in* and *with*. Here's what the passage proclaims:

·　*you have been filled in him* - You have been filled up in Christ with everything you need to be qualified to belong to God. You are absolutely complete before God because you are in his Son. You are God's saint and nothing can change that.

·　*In him also you were circumcised* - Circumcision, as awkward as it is to talk about, was God's chosen symbol to Abraham in the first covenant of inclusion in the household of faith. It signified the cutting away of the sin-filled flesh, of being uniquely branded as God's people. When you came to Christ, you were born from above and given a new heart through the Spirit living in you (called *regeneration*). Your old nature, the flesh, was effectively cut away from you which qualified you to become a member of the body of Christ. The removal of the part of you that stood condemned before God is the analogy pictured here, a circumcision of the heart which is spiritual (Deuteronomy 30:6, Jeremiah 4:4 and Romans 2:29).

· *having been buried with him in baptism* - This is a descriptive picture of the reality that your old sinful self, that part of you that was damned, was not only cut away from you like in circumcision, it was crucified, dead and buried. "Baptism" carries the idea of both the ceremony of declaring your allegiance to Christ through water, and that you are forever and completely identified with him, which is what water baptism symbolizes. In those days, if a boat sank in the sea of Galilee, they would have said the boat was "baptized". When women dyed cloth from the original beige to a beautiful color like purple, they were "baptizing" the cloth. The word baptism carries the idea of a radical change of state. You have been completely immersed into Christ and the Bible says that the real you is actually hidden with Christ. Your soul was "dyed" into Christ and the color change is irreversible.

· *you were also raised with him* - The new you was raised to new life when the Spirit came to live within you, just as the old you was crucified with Jesus' death and buried forever. Because you trust in the stunning power of God, he sees you as raised and seated with his Son in paradise. The only thing that stands between you and that reality coming to fruition is a little bit of time. When thoughts of death and dying make you fearful, focus on your sure position with Christ.

· *God made (you) alive together with him* - This is stating the same truth in another way. God wants to make sure that you fully understand what he has done in you, through your faith in him. Because you are with Jesus in absolute and complete identification, you will not die. In the blink of an eye you will be with him. When life on earth is finished for you, you will live in the breath-taking presence of God for an endless age....*together* with Jesus.

· *having forgiven us all our trespasses* – "Trespasses" is another word for "sins" or "transgressions". You are alive in Christ because every wrong you ever committed (and will commit) was effectively and judiciously nailed to the cross. Every charge against you has been cleared. Your sins were erased because they were put on Jesus and he was punished for them.

How does that help you to understand the spiritual credentials you carry? How do these truths help you to have confidence in who you are in Christ? How do these verses convey the unwavering love your Father has for you?

Each of these truths envelope every single follower of Jesus. The "you" in this passage is plural. This letter was written for the gathered believers in a local church. Embrace these realities for your church family, small group, Bible study and for all of your friends who are in

Christ. Take in these doctrines as being the reality of every Christ-follower on the planet. Think of every believer in this light. See them for who they are in Christ. There is no one in the Kingdom who is more qualified or less qualified than anyone else. There is no place in the Kingdom for comparing, demeaning or elevating. We are all one in Christ and we are all equally endowed with the full credentials of Jesus.

Take Action:

- When you interact with someone who has credentials, remind yourself of your eternal credentialing. Which would you rather have?

- Take time right now to thank God for qualifying you with Jesus' credentials. Thank him for your spiritual certification each time you interact with people who don't yet know him. Pray according to the Kingdom Come Prayer in Ephesians 1:17-19.

To study all of the Kingdom Come Prayers, purchase a copy of my book, *How To Ask God – for What He Wants to Give You* at www.HowToAskGod.com.

READING #9 – DYING TO BE FREE
COLOSSIANS 2:16-23

¹⁶*So don't let anyone condemn you for what you eat or drink, or for not celebrating certain holy days or new moon ceremonies or Sabbaths.* ¹⁷*For these rules are only shadows of the reality yet to come. And Christ himself is that reality.*¹⁸*Don't let anyone condemn you by insisting on pious self-denial or the worship of angels, saying they have had visions about these things. Their sinful minds have made them proud,* ¹⁹*and they are not connected to Christ, the head of the body. For he holds the whole body together with its joints and ligaments, and it grows as God nourishes it.*

²⁰*You have died with Christ, and he has set you free from the spiritual powers of this world. So why do you keep on following the rules of the world, such as,* ²¹*"Don't handle! Don't taste! Don't touch!"?* ²²*Such rules are mere human*

teachings about things that deteriorate as we use them. ²³*These rules may seem wise because they require strong devotion, pious self-denial, and severe bodily discipline. But they provide no help in conquering a person's evil desires.* NLT

"Where is it written?" That's the question that will keep you aligned with Jesus when you are faced with any new teaching, rule, idea or ideal. People are very good at making up their own rules and traditions to try and appease God and/or themselves. So never stop asking yourself: What has God actually said about this? That's why it's so important for you to read the Bible, so that you can renew your thinking, gain God's perspective and be fully prepared when your convictions are challenged.

Have you ever wondered why Jesus so vehemently opposed the religious leaders? What were they doing that was so wrong? Jesus was furious with them because they had taken his Father's commands and added hundreds of their own traditions. They had good intentions. They thought these traditions would help people obey God's commands. But they grossly misapplied God's Word by adding to it. They ended up putting more emphasis on the rules they created than on God's clear commands. That's why Jesus so passionately opposed them, using the most condemning and degrading words possible in warning his listeners not to follow the rules of their religious leaders. (Matthew 23)

The idea that obeying rules and regulations to keep someone in good standing with God is rightly labeled "legalism". Legalism is the idea that a person must do certain things, or never do the forbidden things, in order to remain (*menō*) in God's good graces. Legalism is precisely what Jesus condemned. To add anything to your faith in Christ is a most dangerous sin because it replaces his atoning sacrifice with your personal efforts. God's grace through Jesus' sacrifice is what separates your faith from every other religion. All religions have their unique traditions that were created for the purpose of satisfying God. Instead of purifying the person from sin within, obeying traditions and rules produces pride, which God hates (Proverbs 6:17-19).

My family and I lived in a Muslim country for a number of years. The Muslims I knew were deeply dedicated and religious people. But they based their right standing before God solely on their own ability to carry out the traditions of Islam. A faithful Muslim is as dedicated as they come. Praying five times a day, constantly reciting the creed and the name of Allah, fingering prayer beads throughout the day and fasting during the month of Ramadan are all practices that have the potential of making a person feel very self-righteous. But as the Bible warns in today's passage, none of these actions can change a person's heart. And the core problem with every person on the planet is the condition of their heart. Religion is about keeping rules. Jesus came to give you a relationship with his Father by dealing with the problem of your evil heart.

That is why it is so important for you to continually remind yourself of the warning in vs20-21: *You have died with Christ, and he has set you free from the spiritual powers of this world. Why do you keep on following the rules of the world, such as, "Don't handle! Don' taste! Don't touch!"?* Isn't that a great gut-check question? The freedom from having to try and obey commands and rules in order to be righteous was purchased for you because Jesus obeyed all of God's laws. He then took on the punishment for your disobedience so that you would never have to face God in your own guilt.

If you have come to believe in Jesus and realize that your freedom from God's judgment is in Christ alone, you still have a proclivity to slip back into a performance mentality. Keeping a list of rules will never combat the evil desires that are still part of your physical body, your mind and your heart. No rule can cure the human heart.

Later in this letter, the apostle Paul will teach you how God's people are to live. But it isn't based on keeping rules, it comes from having a new heart. Jesus' transformation process is always from the inside out. He gave you a new heart and is now working on your transformation; the renewing of your thinking and feeling so that your actions and attitudes line up with your new heart. When you first believed in Jesus, a renewal process began by God's Spirit filling your heart and mind with his words and ways. You must be careful to live according to *his* presence and *his* power as you work together to align your thinking with his.

The history of the Church, especially in the U.S., has been severely tainted by man's rules. Every denomination, sad to say, has created spoken and unspoken traditions that are not founded in God's Word. Our current culture is also saturated with liberal rules and values that are far from the kingdom of God. Although they seem good to many people, they are rational lies from the dark domain. Spend some time thinking about this passage by asking yourself what rules, principles, traditions or ideals do you believe and are they truly from God. Where is it written in his Word?

Be very careful that you don't buy into half-truths. The dark kingdom loves to spin God's words by adding a little lie to his truth to make it sound legitimate. Be wary of rational lies. The human mind can rationalize just about anything. Make sure you confirm and affirm what you believe so that your convictions are in complete alignment with Jesus' teachings. Your freedom is based solely on your identification with Christ, in him and him alone.

The highest societal ideals today are tolerance and inclusion. But if an ideal means that sinful choices are tolerated and accepted as normal, that ideal is far from the will of God. Keep asking yourself: "Where is it written?"

Take Action:

- Identify a legalistic teaching or concept that you previously believed. Make sure you have it clear in your mind why forgiveness can never be earned. Why is it based solely on Jesus' atoning sacrifice?

- Instead of rules ruling you, you need Jesus to inhabit your heart. Therefore, pray according to Ephesians 3:16-19. "Father, I ask that from your glorious, unlimited resources, you will empower me with inner strength through your Spirit in the depths of my heart so that Lord Jesus, you will be more and more at home in my heart, and I'll be rooted and grounded in your love, so I will have the strength to understand the vastness of your love and be filled with all of your fullness."

READING #10 – LOOK UP
COLOSSIANS 3:1-4

[1]*If then you have been raised with Christ, seek the things that are above, where Christ is, seated at the right hand of God. [2]Set your minds on things that are above, not on things that are on earth. [3]For you have died, and your life is hidden with Christ in God. [4]When Christ who is your life appears, then you also will appear with him in glory.*
ESV

This is one of the most difficult passages in the Bible to actually live out each day. Read it again in the New Living Translation and let the words sink in.

[1]*Since you have been raised to new life with Christ, set your sights on the realities of heaven, where Christ sits in the place of honor at God's right hand. [2]Think about the*

things of heaven, not the things of earth. ³*For you died to this life, and your real life is hidden with Christ in God.* ⁴*And when Christ, who is your life, is revealed to the whole world, you will share in his glory.* NLT

Do you hear the apostle Paul's plea? "Keep looking up!" Your new life in Christ, no matter how long you have been a follower, is all about acquiring the value system of the Lord Jesus. You are learning to value what he values. How is it possible to keep thinking heavenward in a world that is drenched with responsibilities, demands and obligations, not to mention all the really fun things there are to do? Because you have been raised to new life with Jesus, your perspective about everything is being renewed by your Father in the heavens.

Do you remember the night when Jesus came to the disciples walking on the water and Peter asked to join him? Jesus, probably smiling from ear to ear, said "Come on!" Peter got out of the boat and walked on the water, at least for a few steps. He was resisting all the laws of nature until he thought about the wind against his face and the waves beneath his feet. When he took his eyes off of Jesus and focused on the things around him, he began to sink. Don't you think Jesus was still smiling as he took Peter by the hand and said, "Little faith, why did you doubt?" (Matthew 14:22-33)

The term, "little faith", seemed to be how Jesus both challenged and teased his disciples. He used the phrase as more of an admonishment than a rebuke. It could be compared to how you might encourage someone to think harder when they make a silly mistake by saying, "Way to go Einstein!"

Just like Jesus did to Peter, he gives you the opportunity to live an amazing life and do incredible things as you set your sights on what is above. Don't plan on impressing your friends at the lake by walking on water. But do anticipate making a Kingdom impact at your church and through your work, school and relationships as you keep looking up.

The challenge before you is to not set your full attention on the things around you. Keep looking up. And when you catch yourself focusing on how hard the wind is blowing or how quickly the waves are approaching, look up. Instead of thinking about the person or situation that is making you tense or angry, think about who Jesus is, and what he may be up to in and through you. Keep playing and replaying Jesus' words in your heart and head. There are many voices vying for your attention. Make sure Jesus has the mic so that you are listening to him more than anyone else. *"Seek first the kingdom of God."* (Matthew 6:33-34)

Seeking first the kingdom of God is an amazing concept, but it sure can be difficult to apply. What does seeking the kingdom of God first and foremost in your life really look like and why should you do it? After all, it's much easier to keep focusing on all the stuff here below, just like everybody else. And let's face it, there are some very cool things here below. So let's think about the "why" first.

Paul gave the answer in v1 and vs3-4. He made a "look up" sandwich by placing it in between two slices of whole-doctrine bread. First, you have been raised with Christ Jesus. It is a fact, just as was first stated in 2:12, that you are so completely identified with Jesus that you are effectively seated with him in the heavenlies even now. Why should you have a heavenly perspective about life down here? Because you are just as much up there as you are down here.

You were raised with Christ because you died with Christ (v3 & 2:20). The part of you that stood condemned before God the Almighty was crucified with Jesus. It is dead, buried and gone forever. The whole space and time continuum makes that difficult to believe but believe it you must. Who you really are is now *hidden with Christ in God*. You are so inseparably united with Christ that you are absolutely secure in all of God's promises. The full reality of who you are is not yet visible here on earth, but you are nonetheless with him and in him. When Jesus does return, you will get to share in his spectacularly stunning glory as he rights every wrong and recreates the world to be our new forever home. Part of looking up is to remind yourself continually of the powerful doctrine of v4: *Christ, who is your life!*

Because Christ is your life, a constant dialogue with God is essential. The Kingdom Come prayer you learned from 1:9-12 (pg.7) is a very practical way to set your mind on where Christ is ruling. Use it in quiet times of reading, reflection and meditation as well as in the heat of the battle as a flare player.

You don't have to live like everyone else. Their lives are totally consumed with: careers, degrees, relationships, possessions, habits, problems, abilities, disabilities, sports, diseases, looks, size, memberships, where they live now, where they want to live later, etc. That is not true for you so stop living like it is. Look up! And keep looking up (except when you're driving, then just glance up occasionally). When you get overwhelmed by life's challenges and burdens, remind yourself that you are not of this world. Stop focusing on the wind and how hard it's blowing. Don't keep looking down at your wet feet or listening for the crashing of the waves. Set your sights on the kingdom of God and everything that you need, and need to do in this world today, will fall into place. Look up and trust the One who has absolute authority over everything that is seen and unseen. Develop the habit of taking control of your thinking so you can set your mind on the things above rather than the stuff around you. *³For you have died, and your life is hidden with Christ in God.* You are merely passing through this life, headed full steam ahead to your real life.

Take Action:

- It may be a good practice to actually look up, regardless if it's sunny, cloudy or nighttime, and try and picture Jesus and the Father surrounded by millions of saints and angels in paradise. Remind yourself that you too will be there one day.

- As you look up, speak up. Praying according to 1:9-12 (pg.7) is how you put into practice seeking the things above. Ask the Father to fill you with the full knowledge of his will for what you are facing and to strengthen you with all of his glorious power. Develop the habit of flaring this prayer to your all-knowing Father before meetings, phone calls, answering emails and planning your day.

READING #11 – RENEWING THE NEW YOU
COLOSSIANS 3:5-11

5Put to death, therefore, whatever belongs to your earthly nature: sexual immorality, impurity, lust, evil desires and greed, which is idolatry. 6Because of these, the wrath of God is coming. 7You used to walk in these ways, in the life you once lived. 8But now you must also rid yourselves of all such things as these: anger, rage, malice, slander, and filthy language from your lips. 9Do not lie to each other, since you have taken off your old self with its practices 10and have put on the new self, which is being renewed in knowledge in the image of its Creator. 11Here there is no Gentile or Jew, circumcised or uncircumcised, barbarian, Scythian, slave or free, but Christ is all, and is in all.
NIV

Since v5 begins with a "therefore", read again vs1-4 from Reading #10: *Since, then, you have been raised with Christ, set your hearts on things above, where Christ is, seated at the right hand of God. Set your minds on things above, not on earthly things. For you died, and your life is now hidden with Christ in God. When Christ, who is your life, appears, then you also will appear with him in glory.* NIV

These four verses encapsulate the magnificent truths Paul articulated in Chapters 1 and 2. Now read vs5-11 again, thinking about them from the context of vs1-4.

Because you have been made new *in* Christ, you are constantly being renewed *by* Christ, through his Spirit's work in you. To this point in the letter, Paul presented rich doctrinal truths about Jesus Christ and his people. From this point forward, the letter shifts from conveying God's truths to describing how God's people, who are enveloped in those truths, must strive to live. Beginning in 3:5, the practical aspects of living in God's will day in and day out are clearly presented.

The first command is that you are to *put to death, therefore, whatever belongs to your earthly nature.* The earthly nature is the part of you that was crucified and buried with Christ. The reason you still carry some of those tendencies is because you still live in a mortal body. The effects of your old earthly nature are still in you because sin propensities remain embedded in your physical body. You are to murder each of these temptations every time they arise, by God's grace and with his mighty strength. They are listed: *sexual immorality, impurity, lust, evil desires and greed, which is idolatry. Do not lie to each other...*

There is no place for any form of sexual impurity in God's kingdom. That means there is to be no adultery, pre-marital sex, heavy petting, sexual flirting, homosexuality, bisexuality, cross-dressing, transsexual activity or pornography. God's people are to honor human life as sacred. Sexual sins are incredibly pervasive in our culture and you're bombarded with them every day. What's worse is our culture now accepts many sexual sins as normal, entitled behavior. What God judges as sexual sins are considered as personal rights in today's society. Tolerance is the highest value.

God created sexual intimacy to be enjoyed within the sacred covenant of marriage between a man and a woman. Everything outside of that God judges as a sexual sin that defies his design for his people. There are many passages that speak to this. One of the most articulate passages addressing the sin of homosexuality is Romans 1:18-32. In today's passage in Colossians, the sins listed with sexual sins are interrelated. Evil desires, greed and lying are rooted in sexual immorality, impurity and lust.

What is God's solution for temptations to sexual sins? Kill them! Whenever the temptation comes, murder the idea. Flee the moment. Cry out according to the request in 1:11 (pg.7) and ask your Father to strengthen you with all power according to his glorious might so that you can put the thought to death. Do not play with the idea. Stop thinking about it and murder it! Ask your Father to fill you with the full understanding of his will so that your heart's eyes are wide open to how he views that particular temptation to sexual sin. You must take up this battle because you have been made a warrior of holiness in Christ. Paul reminded you in v7 that you used to live this way but no more. The old you is done and the new you is being renewed by God. You are his beloved, Christ's ambassador everywhere you go and in everything you do.

Like dirty wet clothes, v8 commands you to throw off the leftovers of your old nature such as: *anger, rage, malice, slander, and filthy language* (v8). Do you see how these five sins are interrelated? You must deal with small outbursts of anger before they escalate into rage, malice and slander that produces filthy language. Again, these sins are especially rooted in the sexual sins in vs5-7.

Maybe you don't have to wrestle frequently with these kinds of temptations. If not, thank your Father in the heavens. And realize that the potential is still in you. The only thing lacking is the opportunity. Be fully aware of the potential that resides within your mortal body to commit terrible sins. To combat the old nature's inclinations to sin, you must be intentional.

Commit yourself to renewing the new you. Keep God's words in your heart. Think about his promises. The worst thing you could do is to take the new you for granted and assume you're good to go. You are not. You and every follower of Jesus on the planet needs continual renewal in their hearts and minds. Continue feeding your soul from the Bible, sermons and books and Biblically sound music. Avoid the things that are far from God's ways and be careful which movies and TV shows you watch. Be wise about the people you hang out with and the sites you visit on the web. Keep asking yourself: What or who is currently having the greatest influence on me?

The new you is *being renewed in the knowledge of the image of its Creator* (v10). Wait, read that sentence again. The word for "knowledge" has a special prefix that makes it "full and complete" knowledge and understanding. God is helping you to know him better so that you become more and more devoted *to* him and appreciative *of* him. He is restoring you to be like his Son, nothing less will do. He will not give up renewing you. The way you cooperate in this process is to rely on him to help you put sexual sins and greed to death and to throw off anger and all that is associated with it.

There is one last verse to consider. Why did the Spirit inspire Paul to write v11 here? It is through being renewed by God, as his newly created person, that you can realize how all followers are equal in Christ. There are no cultural, educational, race or economic tiers in the Kingdom. No one is better or less valuable than anyone else and everyone needs to be constantly renewed. We are, of course, at different places in our spiritual maturity, but that too is by the grace of God of which *Christ is all and in all.* All that is good in every follower comes to them directly from the Father. They can take no credit. Instead of considering yourself better or worse than another disciple, realize that both of you are *hidden with Christ in God* (3:3) and in need of regular renewal.

Take Action:

- Spend time thanking God that he has made you new and that he loves you just the way you are today. He loves you so much that he will not let you stay this way. He will keep renewing you.

- Confess each time you follow the temptations of the old you, being very specific with your Father, for your own sake.

READING #12 – DRESS TO KILL
COLOSSIANS 3:12-14

12*Therefore, God's chosen ones, holy and loved, put on heartfelt compassion, kindness, humility, gentleness, and patience,* 13*accepting one another and forgiving one another if anyone has a complaint against another. Just as the Lord has forgiven you, so you must also forgive.* 14*Above all, put on love — the perfect bond of unity.* HCSB

Wearing new clothes that look really great on you builds your confidence. Why? Because good looking, well fitted clothes bring out the best in your outward appearance which effects how you feel about yourself. That's why God chose the illustrative language of "putting on". Putting on the nature of Jesus will radically improve how you feel about yourself and how others perceive you. Paul said the same thing a few verses earlier: *put on the new self* (v10a, pg.63). All of your outward actions and attitudes come from how you look and feel inside, from *who* you are wearing. Are you putting on the new ways of the Kingdom, the influence of the Spirit on you, or the old ways of the dark world? Putting on the new you is how you kill the leftovers of your old nature.

Since being rescued from the dark domain, your life is now about how God is transforming you through a continual renewal process (CRP). The rest of 3:10 (pg. 63) explains God's goal for you: *You are being renewed in knowledge according to the image of your Creator.* God is developing in you the very characteristics of his most beloved Son. This is what he means by *according to the image of your Creator.* So why should you give yourself completely to God's work of making you into the same kind of person that Jesus was?

You have been chosen by God (elected), set apart for him (made holy) and are genuinely loved by him. He not only loves you, the Father likes you! Each one of those truths is amazing in and of itself. Deep within, you know that you didn't deserve him to choose you and you certainly don't deserve his continual love. But you are holy and deeply loved because your Father has forever united you to his Son through your faith. Now that you have been united with Christ Jesus, the rest of your life is about *being renewed in knowledge* into his very nature, which is described in vs12-13.

Let's consider each characteristic listed so you will know how you can most effectively participate with God in your continual renewal process.

· *heartfelt compassion* – an emotional, caring desire to help those whose lives are hurting and broken. You want to show the other person mercy because you feel compassion for them and that is just what they need. Your strength to show this mercy comes from God (1:11-12, pg.10) and is based solely on the compassion you've received from the Lord.

· *kindness* – this is being ready and willing to do good to someone, even if they don't deserve it. Being kind like Jesus will be especially powerful when you extend it to someone who isn't very kind to others. Again, it's based on the amount of kindness God has shown you and it comes from his strength operating within your new heart (1:11-12). Be kind for his sake, not yours or theirs.

· *humility* – the opposite is pride. Remember what God says about all forms of pride. He hates them! Jesus came as a servant, so it makes perfect sense that being united with him means you are also a servant. On the their final trip to Jerusalem, the twelve were arguing about who was the greatest. Jesus told them, *"If anyone wants to be first, he must be last of all and servant of all."* (Mark 9:35). You can't do that on your own. Heck, you probably don't even want to do that most of the time. That is why 3:1-4 (pg.57) is so critical. You must keep your desires on the things above, fixing your mind on Jesus. Continually ask him to fill your thoughts with his understanding (1:9-10, pg.7). If you are humble, will you be taken advantage of? Sure, just like Jesus was. The more you focus on God's greatness, the easier it is to be humble and not take yourself so seriously.

· *gentleness* – this may be a tough characteristic for many men to want to have. It seems soft and weak. Think of it as a no-strings-attached way of encouraging others. It is power in control. Is God harsh or gentle with you? Put on gentleness in how you respond to people because that is part of the delicious fruit of the Spirit of Jesus who is in you, busily renewing you. What did your last harsh response produce anyway?

· *patience* – the word can also be translated: endurance, tolerance, longsuffering, steadfastness, perseverance, forbearance and constancy. When you give this to others, it will probably cost you something. Be ready for that and rely on God's strength to endure (1:11-12, pg.10). The idea is that you are so slow in seeking vengeance that you never do. How patient has God been with you? Accept that we're all cracked pots and just a little bit crazy. You are too. If you don't think so, ask your friends.

· *accepting* – this is similar to being patient in that you know all of the person's weaknesses and short-comings and you overlook them. You bear with them instead of being a bear to them. Because God accepts you with all of your warts and quirks, you must also accept and bear with others in the same way that God accepts you, and them. Rely on the power of God within you to help you focus on Jesus' agape love rather than the things that annoy you about that person. However, this does not mean that you shrink back from confronting them about their sins. You are learning to accept them for who they are and how they are.

· *forgiving* – you will learn to let go of every complaint you have against other people, not clinging to a single one. You can forgive as you seek first to live in the rule and realm of Jesus' forgiving kingdom. According to his vividly descriptive illustration in Matthew 18:21-35, God forgave you of a $16 billion debt that you owed him in order that you can forgive the person who owes you $20 thousand. The comparative ratio is 800,000 to 1! Think about that each time you struggle forgiving someone who owes you an apology, an email, a text or loyalty. *Just as the Lord has forgiven you, so you must also forgive* (v13a). Remember, forgiveness is not an option for you!

·   *agape love* – above every other characteristic, love selflessly and freely. Agape love does not demand love in return. Agape love will always cost you something: time, energy, emotions, money, respect… it always costs. Agape love is the primary characteristic of Jesus because he *is* agape love. You have his agape love in you through the indwelling Spirit of Jesus. By the power and grace of God, his agape love in you will tie all of the other characteristics together in perfect harmony. If you try to be kind or humble or patient without first putting on agape love, you will not succeed. Clothe yourself in the love of Jesus every day and throughout the day using the Kingdom Come Prayer found in Philippians 1:9-11.

Take Action:

- Make the Philippians 1:9-11 prayer your own: "Father, make my agape love overflow more and more in full knowledge and sharp discernment so that I will be able to determine what is best in every situation and be blameless before you every day until the day that you return, and so that I will be filled with the fruit of righteousness that comes through you Lord Jesus, to your glory and for your praise."

READING #13 – GROWING IN THANKFULNESS
COLOSSIANS 3:15-17

15And let the peace of Christ rule in your hearts, to which indeed you were called in one body. And be thankful. 16Let the word of Christ dwell in you richly, teaching and admonishing one another in all wisdom, singing psalms and hymns and spiritual songs, with thankfulness in your hearts to God. 17And whatever you do, in word or deed, do everything in the name of the Lord Jesus, giving thanks to God the Father through him. ESV

Each of these three verses admonish you to be thankful. It's easier to be complacent than to remain continually thankful to God. What's the solution? To this point in the letter, Paul articulated incredibly glorious truths about how God lovingly lavishes his grace on believers. The Father of your Lord Jesus Christ has piled his goodness and grace on you by calling you out of the *dark domain* and into *the kingdom of his beloved Son* (1:13-15, pg.7). He guards you with his power and smothers you in his grace every single day. You *should* be wildly thankful to God every moment of your life.

But that's not how life works, is it? Your world is harsh and full of heartaches. You face challenges and set backs every day. Your Father, who calls you his beloved, knows every temptation you face and all of your disappointments that steal away your thankfulness. And he is always present, ready to help you overcome all of the junk of your old nature, all of the pressures from the world and every whisper from the Evil One.

Because you are in Christ, you have the choice to let the peace of Christ be the ruling authority in your heart. Remember, this letter was first and foremost written to the entire church in Colossae. The letter was read to them collectively. The command was for all of the believers, together, to let the peace of Christ rule over them and among them. It is no different in your church or your small group. Together, we are to help each other experience the joy of our salvation in thankfulness to our Father as we live in peace with God and with each other.

In 1:20 (pg.14), you were reminded that Jesus reconciled heaven and earth by bridging the great divide between his holy Father and rebellious mankind by *making peace by the blood of his cross*. His cross also reconciled the deep divisions between believers by making all of us one in him. We are completely equal in value and importance. The ground *is* level at the foot of the cross. Therefore, you are to do all that you can to let the peace of Christ rule over the divisions that arise in your church or among believers that you know. You can be the catalyst of reconciliation between bickering believers by reminding them that they are one in Christ. Be bold to do all you can to bring the peace of Jesus into your church and among your believing friends. When you are tempted to join in some juicy gossip, resist by the power of God and ask him to fill you, and everyone else, with the full knowledge of his will so that the peace of Jesus pervades.

Because we are all one and there is no pecking order, you are to be deeply thankful: *Let the word of Christ dwell in you richly, teaching and admonishing one another in all wisdom, singing psalms and hymns and spiritual songs, with thankfulness in your hearts to God.* The word of Christ is to inhabit your meetings and your relationships. Everything you do and who you are must be solidly grounded on his Word. The Word not only dwells in every believer, it is to dwell *richly*. In 2:3 (pg.33), the Spirit revealed that *all the treasures of wisdom and knowledge* are hidden in Christ Jesus. Those rich treasures have been revealed to us in God's Word. There is nothing like it on the planet. The words of God are to permeate our conversations, be the basis of every sermon and teaching, and be the center of every song that is sung.

Even though Paul used three different words for music, the original text indicates that the words were synonyms. Think about it this way. Paul was so inspired by the Spirit as he was describing the glorious gathering of believers that he used multiple words to describe the beauty and power of God's saints singing his words back to him. Keeping God's Word dwelling in each believer is how a church can encourage one another to put on compassionate hearts, kindness, humility, meekness, patience and love (3:12-14, pg.69). Proclaiming God's glorious doctrines in your gatherings and worship services will create an atmosphere of authentic praise and thanksgiving.

If your church services, small group meetings or Bible studies don't seem to be as centered on God's Word as this passage instructs, then challenge the leaders to consider these verses.

It's as if Paul was summing up all he had written in the letter to this point when he wrote v17: *And whatever you do, in word or deed, do everything in the name of the Lord Jesus, giving thanks to God the Father through him.* To do everything in the name of Jesus means that you are seeking first his kingdom and you are setting your mind on his Word (v16). Because you now represent Jesus everywhere you go and in everything you do, your entire life is to be lived out from your allegiance to him. As you keep Jesus in mind in all that you think, say and do, you will become a more thankful person. The more you let his peace rule and his Word richly dwell in you, you will experience living in the tangible presence of God (3:1-4, pg.57). There is nothing more joyful than being fully confident that God is always with you and you with him.

Thank God that you have been given Christ's peace. Thank him that his Word is renewing your mind. Thank him that he is helping you, by his grace, in all that you think, say and do. Give thanks to God your Father through Jesus Christ.

Take Action:

- Read the passage again. Now confess specific sins that you have committed including recent times when you failed to put on the attributes described in these verses.

- Make a list of all that you have to be thankful for, remembering that everything good in your life has come to you directly from your Father.

READING #14 – GOD'S BLUEPRINT
COLOSSIANS 3:18-21

[18]*Wives, be submissive to your husbands, as is fitting in the Lord.*

[19]*Husbands, love your wives and don't be bitter toward them.*

[20]*Children, obey your parents in everything, for this pleases the Lord.*

[21]*Fathers, do not exasperate your children, so they won't become discouraged.* HCSB

The family is God's building block for society. He made man and woman in his image by giving each gender his own unique characteristics and brought them together under the covenant of marriage. He created marriage to be a loyal bond between one man and one woman for their lifetime. How far has our society drifted from God's design for the family? In this brief passage, God tells us how he created the family to thrive under his leadership.

Because he chose to make the husband the head of the household, a key responsibility of the wife is to acknowledge God's created order for the family. In every organization, business or team, there must be an authority structure. God chose the husband to lead his wife and the parents to lead their children. His design originated from the Godhead where the Son and the Spirit submit to the Father. They are all equally God, but there is a beautiful order of authority within the Godhead. For husbands, this means that they should strive to be the kind of husband that their wife *wants* to submit to and faithfully follow. It most definitely does not mean that he rules over her, takes advantage of her in any way or neglects his leadership responsibility.

The command for wives to submit to their husbands is extremely unpopular in our culture. It is rejected by so many because God's directive is terribly misunderstood and frequently abused. No one was a greater champion for the value of women (and children) than Jesus Christ. Ephesians 5:22-6:4 is the parallel and expanded teaching on the family where marriage is compared to the relationship between Jesus and his Church. Jesus is the husband and the Church is his bride. Therefore, husbands are to model leading, serving and loving their wives in the same way that Jesus relates to his people, the Church. That is why Colossians 3:19 commands husbands to love their wives with the kind of love that always puts her needs ahead of his. And agape love always costs, so the way you know it's agape is when it cost you something. Agape love is Jesus himself. And since all husbands have the sin-tendency to irritate their wives, God commanded husbands not be bitter or harsh toward them.

Notice in v18 that the wife's submission to her husband should be *fitting in the Lord*. Her first allegiance is to her Lord, so a wife is not held to submit to her husband when he is leading the family contrary to the Lord's words and ways. The basis of her submission is not her husband's worthiness. She honors her husband out of her reverence for the Lord. As the husband's leadership must be rooted in agape love for his wife and children, so must her submission be rooted in respect and admiration for her husband.

The core need of husbands and wives is very different. God created man with the need to be admired and respected (Ephesians 5:33). Notice that he never commanded wives to *love* their husbands. Peter encouraged wives of non-believing husbands to respect them and be subject to them so that they may be won over to the Lord (1 Peter 3:1-6). How much more should the wife of a believing husband be able to respect him? Because men were created by God to work to provide for their family, showing respect for her husband's vocation is a powerful way for the wife to tangibly demonstrate her admiration and submission to him. That's what husbands need!

God created wives with the core need to be loved and cherished (Ephesians 5:25, 33). That is why husbands are commanded to agape love their wives. When a husband coveys authentic agape love, his wife will feel secure emotionally, physically and spiritually. As the husband agape loves and cherishes his wife and the wife honors and respects her husband, God's beautiful blueprint for marriage is realized and the two enjoy the mystery of becoming one.

His plan for marriage pinnacles in the raising of children. What children need more than anything is to be raised by a mom and dad that love and respect each other, and the Lord, by following his design for their marriage and family. Children need to see their parents growing together in unity by God's grace and strength. Remember Colossians 1:18. Jesus is to have first place in your marriage and family, not your spouse and definitely not your kids. Parents are to strive to show their children the same kind of unity that is enjoyed by the Father, the Son and the Spirit.

Realize that children were never made to be worshipped. They can't handle that kind of pressure. No human can. God alone is to be worshipped. Instead, children are to be taught to honor and obey their parents so that they can learn how to honor and worship God. A profound question for a parent to ask is: "What kind of adult do I want my child to grow up to be? Would I want to live beside them when they're twenty five?" Raise them accordingly.

Parents especially love Colossians 3:20. If your child wants to get a tattoo, agree if it's this verse! *Children, obey your parents in everything, for this pleases the Lord.* It's easy to understand God's design for the family when you realize his perspective about children honoring and obeying their parents. Of the Ten Commandments, the first four teach us how to love and respect God and the next six teach us how to relate to one another, in the family and in society. God emphasized the importance of children respecting their parents by this first commandment regarding all human relationships: *Honor your father and your mother, as the LORD your God has commanded you, so that you may live long and so that it may go well with you in the land that the LORD your God is giving you.* (Deuteronomy 4:16, *"LORD"* in Hebrew is *Yahweh*, God's personal and covenantal name.)

Parents are to raise their children so that they learn how to respect and obey authority. When children learn to do that in the home they grow up in, they will very likely carry that reverence for authority into society. Any school teacher can tell you. If a child doesn't show respect in the classroom, it's probably because they don't show respect to their parent(s) at home. Society breaks down when the home breaks down and children are not taught to obey and respect their parent(s).

Lastly, fathers are given an admonition. It is very interesting that mothers are not included in v21. Why is that? God chose to create women with his nurturing characteristics. That's why you ran to your mom when you skinned your knee. Men don't have the same tender love and nurturing nature that women have. Fathers actually have a sin-propensity to frustrate their children. They can do this by demanding too much from them or by expecting them to be something they are not, such as a straight-A student or a star athlete. That is why the Spirit led Paul to admonish all fathers to be careful that they don't frustrate and discourage their sons and daughters.

God's design for families is holy. It is the pinnacle of his entire creation. The idea embraced by society that two men or two women can be happily married and even raise healthy children is radically opposed to God's created order. What happens when you don't have order?

Doing family God's way isn't easy and he never intended us to do it without his help. The two prayer requests in 1:9-12 (pg.7) for wisdom and strength are critical if you want to be the family that Christ intended.

Take Action:

- Because you need God's wisdom in your role as husband, wife or child, ask your Father for his help using the Kingdom Come prayer in Colossians 1:9-12 (pg.7).

- Think about why it makes sense that homosexual relationships are so diametrically opposed to God's basic design of mankind. For God's clear perspective on homosexuality and society, study Romans 1:18-32.

- Think through Genesis 1-2 to get more grounded on the beauty and power of God's created order.

READING #15 – REPORTING TO JESUS
COLOSSIANS 3:22-4:1

²²Bondservants, obey in everything those who are your earthly masters, not by way of eye-service, as people-pleasers, but with sincerity of heart, fearing the Lord. ²³Whatever you do, work heartily, as for the Lord and not for men, ²⁴knowing that from the Lord you will receive the inheritance as your reward. You are serving the Lord Christ. ²⁵For the wrongdoer will be paid back for the wrong he has done, and there is no partiality. ⁴:¹Masters, treat your bondservants justly and fairly, knowing that you also have a Master in heaven. ESV

English Bibles translate *doúlos* as either "slave", "servant" or "bondservant". In the first century, the word denoted compulsory service to a "master" that ranged from owning an individual to working for someone in order to pay back a debt. Sometimes a contract was involved. It was very different than the slavery of African-Americans in the U.S. that we typically picture when we read the word "slave". The application for this passage for us today is clear: God gave us irrefutable instructions about our employer-employee relationships that equally apply to a teacher-student or coach-player relationship. This teaching also governs every other relationship where one person has authority over another.

Read v22 again. How does that make you feel? God expects you to obey your boss out of your reverence and awe (*fear*) for him. He obviously does not intend you to break his holy laws by cheating, stealing or lying. The Lord expects you to be one of the very best employees your boss and company have ever had. Whoever you serve or report to in your job, you are to do so with the utmost integrity and with a stellar work ethic. Strive for excellence in all you do, whether anyone is watching or not, because your Lord sees all you do. Even when your boss is unfair to you, doesn't give you credit or acknowledge your contributions to the company, you are to serve them wholeheartedly at all times.

This can be a very difficult teaching to obey. How do you continue to work hard for someone who treats you so unfairly? How can you faithfully serve on those days when your boss is being a professional jerk? God clears that up for you in vs23-24. His perspective about your work or studies is that you are doing it ALL for him. Yes, you are accountable to a manager or professor, but in actuality you are reporting directly to the Lord Jesus Christ. The way to work with whole-hearted integrity is to continually remind yourself that the Lord is aware of everything you are doing, all day long, and he is the one you are serving. Your work matters to God! The *way* in which you do your work (quality and attitude) is especially important to your heavenly Father. He cares about your most mundane tasks. He wants you to represent his name at your job so that others will praise *him* for how *you* are working.

When a co-worker asks you why you are always on time or why you work so diligently, you are to share with them this truth. Let them know that your relationship with God is such that he wants you to give your absolute best at work because your work is important to him. The last sentence of v24 sums it up beautifully: *You are serving the Lord Christ.* The word for "serving" is the verb form of the noun *doúlos*, from v22. Your relationship with Jesus is friend to friend and servant to master.

When you don't feel like working hard because your boss doesn't appreciate you or your client is being unrealistic or your instructor is showing favoritism, know that Jesus is fully aware. He wants to empower you in the depth of your soul to be able to overcome those feelings with faith in him. It may help you to picture in your mind Jesus sitting at your manager's desk. Whatever helps you to serve the Lord in your job, do that. But know that in everything you do at work, Jesus wants you to do it with your whole heart because you report to him, first and foremost.

God gives you even more motivation to work diligently by reminding you that you have a promised inheritance. The way you serve the Lord in this life will impact your life in the world to come. In the new euphoric world, there will be rewards for faithfulness to Jesus that will come from how you served him in this sin-infested world. That's another reason to work with integrity and to jettison complaining to fellow employees. Your attitude, even with the most boring assignments, matters to the Lord of the cosmos. Isn't that astonishing? If it matters to him, shouldn't it matter to you too? Keep that reality in the forefront of your thinking throughout your workday.

What do you do when you're treated unfairly at work or school? Sing out with Queen Elsa from

Frozen, "Let It Go"! You can let it go by trusting in God who is all-knowing and full of mercy and justice. He assured you in v25 that every wrongdoer will be handled with justice by *the* just and holy Judge. You must never pursue personal vengeance or reciprocate a wrong done to you. You are instructed to trust God and let him take care of all retribution. *You* can let it go knowing that God is trustworthy, righteous and just.

If you are in a job that you don't like, you must continue to work hard and do your absolute best, every day. If you want to find a better job, then look for one. Search and interview as diligently as you can but trust God with the outcome. Realize that he may keep you in a difficult job to grow your faith. Therefore, as long as you are employed you are to serve that employer as if you are directly serving the Lord, because in reality, you are. Work with the integrity of Jesus.

Next, the Lord spoke to all who are employers, coaches, teachers, anyone who has authority over others. Is that you? Read 4:1 again. You are to treat every employee equally with absolute justice and mercy. Treating them with compassion has nothing to do with whether they deserve it or not. They may deserve to be fired on the spot. You are to treat each employee with absolute dignity *knowing you also have a Master in heaven*. Your Master in heaven is full of grace so give 'em grace!

Each employee or student was created in the image of God and is to be treated as such. Your goal is to be the kind of boss or authority figure that brings out the best in those who report to you. Treating your direct reports the same way that Jesus would treat them will inspire them to bring their best to the job. That may not be true for every single person, but it will play out for the majority. Employees are always impacted by the power of God in a boss or manager. Be winsome and let them see Jesus in you. Remember what Christ said about greatness: "*If anyone would be first, he must be last of all and servant of all.*" (Mark 9:35) As a manager of others, your job is to serve them first and foremost. Be the first to admit failure and the last to promote yourself. Give every responsibility and each employee your absolute best. As you faithfully serve those who report to you, you can trust that God will honor your efforts. Keep your mind fixed on the things above instead of promotions, raises and a better benefits package (3:1-4, pg.57). You will need his constant help so continue praying for wisdom and power.

Take Action:

- How do you come across to your boss and peers? What is one attitude change that you need to make so that you really are serving the Lord Jesus at work or at school?

READING #16 – KEEP PRAYING
COLOSSIANS 4:2-4

²Continue steadfastly in prayer, being watchful in it with thanksgiving. ³At the same time, pray also for us, that God may open to us a door for the word, to declare the mystery of Christ, on account of which I am in prison - ⁴that I may make it clear, which is how I ought to speak.
ESV

This short but powerful passage admonishes you to devote yourself to praying. If you don't consider yourself a prayer warrior, then begin moving in that direction today, for that is your Father's desire for you. Verse 2 reveals how you can persevere in prayer. As you incorporate watchfulness and thankfulness into your praying, you *will* become more steadfast. Let's consider how you can live out this verse.

Your heavenly Father, because he loves you with an unwavering devotion, longs for you to become more and more dedicated to him. He definitely wants the relationship to go both ways. He tells you in v2 to persevere in prayer because that is how you will deepen your relationship with him. He longs for your love and your loyalty.

What comes to your mind when you read, *Continue steadfastly in prayer*? How about, *Devote yourselves to prayer*? What would your life look like if others described you as a follower of Jesus who is devoted to praying?

It's not that you have to become a monk and go live in some monastery. Persevering in prayer doesn't mean you have to spend hours in Bible study and prayer every day. Being steadfast means you are continually talking with your Father in the heavens about the things that are important to both of you. You should have some times during the week, preferably daily, when you can be alone in a quiet place, so that you can spend quality time praying, reading and listening to your Father. The more practical side of continuing steadfastly in prayer is having prayer "texts" with your Father throughout the day. Flare praying when you need his help or when you want to thank him for the grace he just gave you *is* steadfast praying.

In 3:1-2 (pg.57), you were taught to seek first the things that are above, where Jesus is reigning, by fixing your mind on the realities of his kingdom. Praying continually is precisely how you focus your thinking on Jesus' kingdom. Having short conversations with your Father throughout the day is how you obey 3:1-2. By being steadfast and devoted to praying you *are* seeking Jesus' will first and you *are* setting your mind on what matters to him. The way to seek first the things above is to talk to the One who *is* above!

The Spirit led Paul to describe how you can continue faithfully praying to your Father. You do it by being watchful and thankful. Pause for a moment and consider how being alert and thankful may help your praying. Being watchful is a metaphor that means to give strict attention to praying while being actively cautious. The idea is that you must be thoughtful and fully aware that your natural tendency is to *not* be attentive to your need for frequent prayer. Your man-made proclivity is to allow the Me Monster within to run the show. Instead, the Spirit wants to inspire you to be aware of your need for his involvement.

To be watchful in praying to the Father means you are alert to when you need God's help. Being watchful is to recognize that if you don't ask for the Father's wisdom and insights, you will not respond in the best way. Results will be less than excellent. When you don't know how to respond or react, be observant that you need your Father's help. When you ask God to fill you with the knowledge of his will in all wisdom and spiritual understanding (1:9, pg.7) and to strengthen you with all power according to his glorious might (1:11), you are being focused and alert. The more you ask the more observant you will become.

Continuing faithfully in prayer is not only to be done attentively, it is to be done with a thankful heart. You will grow in your devotion to the Lord as you become more appreciative of his grace in your life. One of the best ways to deepen your relationship with the Father is to begin to look for things to thank him for. Renew your thinking by paying attention to the wonders of his creation, from the beauty of nature to the diversity of people. You are continuing steadfastly in prayer when you thank him that you avoided an accident, that someone sent you a kind text, that your lab results came back negative, and most importantly, that he chose to make you his son or daughter.

Try this. Only thank God today. Don't ask him to do anything. As you go through your day (or night), thank him for everything that comes to mind. Ask him to help you to realize all of the good that he has brought about in your life. Begin to do this more and more and you will soon develop an attitude of gratitude that will also fuel your desire to pray.

Continual and steadfast praying is kind of like texting. You don't spend your *entire* day texting, unless you're a high schooler! But you have your phone, your network and your friend's number, so you have the ability to text anytime you want. When something good or funny happens, don't you want to share it with someone close to you? And when something disappointing occurs, you need to be consoled by a friend. Your Father loves you so much more than anyone on earth so move towards *him* during your busy day by having short conversations, prayer texts. You will find that as you ask, he will give you the wisdom and insights to respond in ways that make both of you smile. You will experience an inner empowerment to be able to stand on your convictions and not cave in, even when everyone around you falls for the rational lies. By increasing your text-time with your Father, you will most definitely deepen your devotion to him.

It's a fact. We all need God's help. That's why Paul asked the members of Colossae Community Church to pray for God to open doors for him to teach about Christ in a clear and compelling way. That church must have devoted themselves to praying attentively for Paul because God certainly opened many doors. Look at how wide a door this letter came to be! Millions have received Paul's teaching from its pages. That's the power of asking God according to his will.

Ask the same thing for your pastors and others in vocational ministry. All of us are to be ready to tell others about our faith in Jesus in a clear and compelling way. But for those who are ministering vocationally, they have the full-time job of declaring *the mystery of Christ* and certainly need to remain filled with the full knowledge of God's will in all spiritual wisdom and all spiritual understanding. Pray this request for yourself, your friends, your church members and especially for your pastors and leaders.

Take Action:

- Use your regular schedule of activities during the day or night, like commuting, break, lunch, before meetings, after conference calls, before answering emails, etc. to build into your life the habit of continual, devoted praying. Use the Kingdom Come Prayers as your prayer-texts.

- During your devotional time, use Jesus' outline for praying as your guide from Luke 11:1-4. Also read vs5-13 to learn what Jesus taught about persistence and the gift your Father loves to give.

READING #17 – W.A.I.T.
COLOSSIANS 4:5-6

⁵*Walk in wisdom toward outsiders, making the best use of the time.* ⁶*Let your speech always be gracious, seasoned with salt, so that you may know how you ought to answer each person.* ESV

"Outsiders" are those who have not yet received Jesus Christ as the Lord of their lives. You may not be very comfortable thinking about those who don't follow Jesus as "outsiders", but that is who they are. Jesus used the same word in Mark 4:11: *"To you has been given the secret of the kingdom of God, but for those outside everything is in parables…"*.

Jesus doesn't want anyone to be outside of his kingdom. Sadly, millions refuse his offer of forgiveness. Your calling, as an ambassador of the

King and his kingdom, is to show outsiders the same kind of grace and mercy that you were shown when you were an outsider. Who were the saints who led you to come in from the dark? Remember how they acted and how they spoke?

You are instructed to do two things in v5. You are to act wisely toward everyone who does not know Jesus and you are to make the best use of the time you have with them. You are to carefully consider how you are living your life, especially around those who don't yet know Jesus. This command doesn't mean that you have to act perfectly and never make a mistake. One of the most powerful things you can do is to apologize when you sin against them. For example, you might get pulled into the office chatter putting down a fellow employee or a manager. If that happens, go back and apologize for what you said to all who need to hear it.

To be able to act wisely and leverage the opportunities you have, you will need to be filled with the full knowledge of God's will to know how to react and respond. Does that ring a bell? Use the prayer from 1:9-12 (pg.7) to ask the Lord to give you his Spiritual insights so that you can say and do what is wise and appropriate for the moment. Ask him to strengthen you with all power according to his glorious might so that you will have all the endurance you need to live wisely each day, especially when a challenging situation arises. Keep asking your Father to strengthen you in your inner being so that you will have all the patience you need, especially with that outsider that you find so challenging to like. Finally, never stop asking your Father for his strength so that you can be joyful as you live among outsiders, thanking him that he has brought you in from the dark (1:13, pg.10)

Making the best use of your time with those who are far from God can be very intimidating. But you must not feel like you have to walk around on pins and needles out of fear you'll mess up and damn that person to the eternal abyss! Your Father doesn't want you to be afraid of saying or doing the wrong thing. He wants you to live in the freedom that he has purchased for you, relying on his Spirit within you to give you the wisdom you need with just the right words. So relax as you make the most of each opportunity. Rely on him! Your Father wants you to trust in him with confidence that his Spirit will intervene in and through you to bring about his purposes.

This is what life will be like as you seek first and set your mind on the things above (3:1-2, pg.57). It is God himself who will give you the desire to live wisely so that you leverage your time with outsiders. And he will also give you the power to act appropriately, so that they can see Jesus in your actions and hear him through your words (Philippians 2:12-13). Seeking Jesus' perspective first and foremost comes through abiding prayer, like you read about previously in 4:2 (pg.95). Learning to discipline yourself to have on-going conversations with your Father is how you set your mind on his kingdom.

In v6, Paul carried this thought further. Words are very important and very powerful. You can still remember harsh words that deeply wounded you. Hopefully, you can also reflect back to kind and encouraging words that someone with influence spoke to you. This verse commands you to make sure that your words are always filled with grace and mercy towards outsiders. Jesus taught you to be *"wise as serpents and innocent as doves"* (Matthew 10:16b). To do this, you will need God's wisdom and strength flowing through you.

To be careful with words means that you are quick to listen and slow to speak (James 1:19). Make sure you are even slower to text and post! Let your blood pressure return to normal before you give a reply. The acronym W.A.I.T. may help you: Why Am I Talking? Speaking when you are angry or upset can lead to deep wounds that will need multiple apologies. Taking the time and energy to ask your Father for his help will keep you from speaking too quickly.

One of the most powerful things you can do to another person is to genuinely listen to them. This is especially true of outsiders who may think you want to cram your faith down their throat. Before you ever talk to them about your faith in Jesus, show them the agape love of Jesus. Value them as a person who was made in the image of God and seek to hear their heart.

Paul illustrated wise words as being *seasoned with salt*. Salt was widely used in the ancient world as a religious symbol of endurance and value. It was their primary preservative as well as a popular seasoning. Just the right amount of salt can have an amazing impact on a meal but too much will ruin it. It's similar with your words. That is why you are instructed by God to be careful with *what* you say, *when* you say it and *how* you say it. Make sure you are hearing the other person first. They need to *feel* like they've been heard. When it is time for you to talk, sense the Spirit's help as you rely on his power and wisdom to speak deliciously seasoned words.

Peter was inspired in a similar way: *but in your hearts honor Christ the Lord as holy, always being prepared to make a defense to anyone who asks you for a reason for the hope that is in you; yet do it with gentleness and respect...* (1 Peter 3:15). Again, the way to tell someone about your hope in Christ with gentleness and respect is to be filled with the

Spirit as you share. How do you get filled with the Spirit? Ask and keep on asking for the Father to fill you with the full knowledge of his will in all spiritual wisdom and spiritual understanding. His Spirit will guide your spirit to have all the wisdom, love, gentleness and respect that you will need. Rely on your Father by staying in constant contact with him. Then you will live worthy of the Lord, fully pleasing him, and your life will produce fruit that lasts. You will also grow in your understanding of God the Almighty. Staying in touch with the Father through prayer will result in the words of Christ dwelling richly in you and pouring out to your friends and colleagues who don't yet know him. That is how you can make *the best use of your time* and seize the day.

Take Action:

- Flare prayer the 1:9 (pg.7) request to your Father as you get into conversations with outsiders, whether you talk about spiritual things or not.

- Study the prayer in Philippians 1:9-11 and begin asking the Father to make your love overflow more and more in knowledge and discernment. Focus on this prayer's results in vs10-11.

READING #18 – GOD KNOWS NAMES
COLOSSIANS 4:7-18

[7]*Tychicus will tell you all about my activities. He is a beloved brother and faithful minister and fellow servant in the Lord.* [8]*I have sent him to you for this very purpose, that you may know how we are and that he may encourage your hearts,* [9]*and with him Onesimus, our faithful and beloved brother, who is one of you. They will tell you of everything that has taken place here.*

[10]*Aristarchus my fellow prisoner greets you, and Mark the cousin of Barnabas (concerning whom you have received instructions—if he comes to you, welcome him),* [11]*and Jesus who is called Justus. These are the only men of the circumcision among my fellow workers for the kingdom of God, and they have been a comfort to me.* [12]*Epaphras, who is one of you, a servant of Christ Jesus, greets you, always struggling on your behalf in his prayers, that you*

107

may stand mature and fully assured in all the will of God. *13For I bear him witness that he has worked hard for you and for those in Laodicea and in Hierapolis. 14Luke the beloved physician greets you, as does Demas. 15Give my greetings to the brothers at Laodicea, and to Nympha and the church in her house. 16And when this letter has been read among you, have it also read in the church of the Laodiceans; and see that you also read the letter from Laodicea. 17And say to Archippus, "See that you fulfill the ministry that you have received in the Lord."*

18I, Paul, write this greeting with my own hand. Remember my chains. Grace be with you. ESV

Why should you spend time reading about these people with weird names who lived almost 2,000 years ago? How can it help you to know that Nympha hosted a church in her home or that Jesus (Paul's team member) was also called Justus? The reason these people are mentioned by name is because each one of them mattered to God. They were all uniquely chosen by the Father, adopted into his family and given abilities, Spiritual giftedness and uniquely specific responsibilities in his kingdom. These names are to remind you that they were the first members of Christ's Church worldwide and that just as God called and equipped them, he has been calling and equipping his saints since that time, all over the world and from all walks of life. These names are a vivid reminder that he called you and is equipping you to do the Kingdom work he has uniquely created you to do (Eph 2:8-10).

Think about the diverse team that worked with Paul to spread the fantastic news (the gospel) about Jesus throughout that region of the world.

·   *Tychicus* was one of Paul's most trusted emissaries who delivered his letters to the churches in Colossae and Ephesus. He was with Paul until his death (2 Tim 4:12).

·   *Onesimus* was a runaway slave who apparently came to faith in Christ through Paul's ministry in Rome. Philemon was his owner and was a member of the church in Colossae. On his trip to Colossae, Tychicus delivered Paul's letter to the church and his letter to Philemon. He urged Philemon to forgive Onesimus and to receive him as a brother in Christ rather than as a runaway slave (Philemon 1:1-25).

·   *Aristarchus* had been traveling with Paul since joining him in Ephesus (Acts 19:29) and was now a prisoner with him. Just because Paul wrote little about him, doesn't mean he was less valuable. Are you in the spot light or back stage? Can you picture how Aristarchus may have encouraged Paul as he wrote the Prison Epistles?

·   *Mark* traveled with Paul and Barnabas on the first missionary journey. But Mark left them during the trip and Paul was so upset that he would not allow Mark to rejoin him on the second journey. That is when Paul and Barnabas separated (Acts 15:37-40) and went their separate ways, with Mark joining Barnabas. But the power of Christ's agape love reconciled Paul and Mark and 10 years later Paul wrote about how very useful Mark was for ministry (2 Tim 4:11). Mark, also called John Mark, was the author of the Gospel of Mark. Never doubt the power of Jesus to reconcile believers. Do you need to be reconciled to another follower?

· *Jesus*, which was a common name in the first century, was also called *Justus*. Think about this man. The Spirit did not inspire Paul to say anything more about him, except to include him as a Jewish team member who, like the others listed, was a *fellow worker for the kingdom of God* and a *comfort* to Paul (v11). He was a backstage hand who faithfully served as God enabled him, but was never in man's spot light.

· *Epaphras* was the founding pastor of the church in Colossae who met with Paul to share how the church was doing and the challenges it was facing. We learn of his heart for his home town people (v12) as well as his love for his fellow believers in the neighboring cities of Laodicea and Hierapolis. Why don't more parents name their sons "Epaphras"? He must have had a special calling by God to pray for fellow believers. You may not be branded as a "prayer warrior" like Epaphras apparently was, but you can also struggle on behalf of those you pray for, that they *may stand mature and fully assured in all the will of God.*

· *Luke* was Paul's especially faithful companion and chronicler. He recorded most of Paul's letters, excluding some of the salutations (v18), and also wrote the Gospel of Luke and Acts. He was exceptionally literate but being a physician does not mean he was a man of high social standing. In those days, many physicians were slaves.

· *Demas* is a warning to you. He was apparently faithful during the writing of this letter but later abandoned Paul because of his *love with this present world* (2 Tim 4:10). Paul no doubt saw this happen to many believers as he urged the saints in Romans 12:1-2 to be a *living sacrifice, holy and acceptable to God* and to not be *conformed to this world but be transformed by the renewal* of their minds. Don't be a Demas! And yes, it is a play on words!!

· *Nympha* was a woman in Laodicea who hosted the church in her home. Since her husband isn't mentioned, she was probably a widow. There is no evidence of churches owning buildings until the middle of the third century. The early churches typically met in homes.

·   *Archippus* is a bit of a mystery. We don't know if he was dodging his God-given ministry responsibilities or if Paul took this opportunity to encourage him in his role as co-pastor with Epaphras. Either way, here was a man who had been given a specific ministry from the Lord that was important to the health of the entire church. Pastors and leaders need special prayer and encouragement because their ministry is influential to so many. Pray continually for your pastor(s) and leaders according to 1:9-12 (pg.7). Encourage them every chance you get. They definitely need it!

The veracity of the Bible is proven once again in v16. The letter Paul wrote to the church in Laodicea was not inspired by God. The Lord did not protect and preserve that letter like he did Paul's letters to the churches in Rome, Corinth, Galatia, Ephesus, Philippi, Colossae and Thessalonica (as well as his personal letters to Timothy, Titus and Philemon). We have no copies of a letter from Paul to the church in Laodicea because it was not God's divinely inspired Word. The letter was no doubt helpful to the church and true to the faith, but not God-breathed (2 Timothy 3:16). Be encouraged that your Bible is indeed God's divinely inspired Word. Jesus said that you will remain (*menó*) in him as his words remain (*menó*) in you (John 15:1-11). The old apostle John wrote that you will remain (*menó*) in the Son and the Father if the truth remains (*menó*) in you (1 John 2:24-25). Continue reading his holy Word. *Let the word of Christ dwell in you richly* (3:16, pg.75) so that you can apply it to every situation you face. As you continue (*menó*) in his words, you will grow in your devotion to your heavenly Father who loves you with an everlasting love.

Take Action:

- Spend time reviewing your favorite passages in Colossians. How have these readings helped you to *stand mature and fully assured in all the will of God* (v12)? How will you continue?

- Epaphras prayed earnestly for his fellow believers to be mature and faithful to follow the whole will of God. Own the prayer of 1:9-12 (pg.7) and pray that way for yourself and others.

Thank you for reading Take 10 to Menó. Please let me know how these readings have helped you. Contact me at Take10toMeno.com. *May the God of hope fill you with all joy and peace in believing, so that by the power of the Holy Spirit you may abound in hope.* Romans 15:13 ESV

ABOUT THE AUTHOR

Bill and his wife, Tammy, grew up in bustling metropolis of Fuquay-Varina, NC. They were married in 1981 after Bill graduated from NC State's School of Engineering. A few months after their marriage, Bill became a follower of Jesus. After eight years of success in business, the Simpsons realized the Lord was leading them in a radically new direction. They sold their home and company in order to attend seminary at Columbia International University in Columbia, SC. After graduation, Bill served as the country field director and lead church planter for six years in Senegal, West Africa with the mission organization, SIM. In their last year in Senegal, Bill was inspired to write his first book. It explained basic theology in the Wolof language using indigenous illustrations and parables. After the Simpsons returned to the US in 1997, Bill was privileged to serve as the senior pastor of their home church in High Point, NC, Community Bible Church. He ministered there for almost 10 years and then returned to his second vocational love, engineering. Bill and Tammy were led back to the pastorate five years later as he became the Senior Pastor of Manchester Creek Community Church in Rock Hill, SC. He resigned after four years to pursue a full-time writing ministry. In addition to this book, Bill has also written a devotional book, published a podcast, writes articles for numerous publications, and is currently working on a new book, *What Men Crave – and It's Not Money, Sex, and Power.* His passion is to bring clarity and confidence to the people of God. Discover additional resources at www.BillSimpson.org.

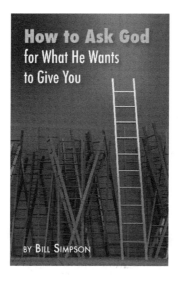

Bill's second book, *How to Ask God – for What He Wants to Give You*, brings a fresh and easy-to-read perspective on praying. This book teaches, directly from the Bible, how God wants you to pray and what he wants you to ask him to do. Jesus taught that if we remain (*menō*) in him and his words remain (*menō*) in us, we can ask for whatever we want and it will happen! Learn how Jesus' promise can become your daily experience. You will also learn how to use Jesus' outline for praying and how to own the Kingdom Come Prayers. You can purchase the books at Amazon or any on-line book retailer or through the website, www.HowToAskGod.com. It's an excellent resource for small groups and Bible studies, as well as an engaging devotional for couples. Each chapter concludes with five discussion questions. A free Leader's Guide is also available on the website.

Drive Time Devotionals is a podcast of practical and applicable biblical teaching by Bill. Each episode is about 10 minutes long, just right for your commute to work or time on the treadmill. You can listen to the DTD podcast on iTunes, Spotify, Google Play, or Sketcher.

COLOSSIANS

TAKE 10 TO MENÓ